JN

‑|90

D0571037

The
New York Colony

by Dennis B. Fradin

Consultant: Wendell Tripp, Ph.D.
New York State Historical Association
Cooperstown, New York

 CHILDRENS PRESS ®
CHICAGO

Acknowledgment

For their help, the author thanks:

Dr. Wendell Tripp, New York State Historical Association

Wilhelmina Prins-Koeller, Press and Cultural Affairs Officer, Consulate General of The Netherlands, Chicago, Illinois

Library of Congress Cataloging-in-Publication Data

Fradin, Dennis B.
  The New York Colony.

  Includes index.
  Summary: Traces the history of the Dutch colony beginning with the years it was inhabited only by Indians to the time it became the eleventh state. Includes biographical sketches on famous New Yorkers such as Hiawatha, Peter Minuit, and Captain Kidd.
    1. New York (State)—History—Colonial period, ca. 1600-1775—Juvenile literature. 2. New York (State)—History—Colonial period, ca. 1600-1775—Biography—Juvenile literature. 3. New York (State)—History—Revolution, 1775-1783—Juvenile literature. 4. New York (State)—History—Revolution, 1775-1783—Biography—Juvenile literature. 5. New York (State)—Biography—Juvenile literature. [1. New York (State)—History—Colonial period, ca. 1600-1775. 2. New York (State)—History—Revolution, 1775-1783. 3. New York (State)—Biography] I. Title.
F122.F83 1988   974.7'02   87-35803
ISBN 0-516-00389-5

Table of Contents

Ships sail past the Statue of Liberty during bicentennial celebrations in New York Harbor, 1976.

Chapter I

Introducing the Empire State

*We were much gratified on arriving in this country:
Here we found beautiful rivers, bubbling fountains
flowing into valleys, basins of running waters in the
flatlands, agreeable fruits in the woods . . .
considerable fish in the rivers, good tillage land. . . .*

*Present-day New York is described in 1624
by one of its first colonists*

Shaped somewhat like an Indian arrowhead, New York State is located in the northeastern United States. New York is bounded by Canada and Lake Ontario to the north; the states of Vermont, Massachusetts, and Connecticut to the east; the Atlantic Ocean and New Jersey and Pennsylvania to the south; and Pennsylvania, Lake Erie, and Canada to the west.

New York City, the United States' largest city, is in southeastern New York State. New York City is home to more than seven million people—more than the population of Los Angeles and Chicago (the nation's second and third largest cities) combined. Because people of various colors, religions, and national backgrounds live there, New York City has been called a "melting pot."

One of the best-known of New York City's many famous landmarks is the Statue of Liberty, the huge symbol of freedom in New York Harbor. Among the city's other attractions are the United Nations, the Brooklyn Bridge, the Empire State Building, two major league baseball teams (the Yankees and Mets), Central Park, the Bronx Zoo, and many famous museums, including the Metropolitan Museum of Art. New York City's Broadway area is the country's most famous theater district, and Wall Street its most famous financial district.

New York City has more publishers than any other American city. It is also the country's main center for radio and TV broadcasting. Among the major networks headquartered there are the American Broadcasting Company (ABC), the Columbia Broadcasting System (CBS), and the National Broadcasting Company (NBC).

The state has much to offer besides New York City. It has several other good-sized cities, including Buffalo (the state's second biggest city), Rochester, Yonkers, Syracuse, and Albany (the capital). The state has hundreds of lovely small towns and beautiful scenery.

United Nations headquarters (above). The Brooklyn Bridge (below)

Niagara Falls

Forests of ash, birch, maple, spruce, white pine, and other trees cover about 60 percent of the state. New York also has several impressive mountain ranges, including the Catskills in the southeast and the Adirondacks in the northeast.

The Hudson, the St. Lawrence, the Susquehanna, and the Mohawk are four of the rivers that wind through New York. In places where the ground suddenly drops in height, some of the rivers form waterfalls. North America's most famous waterfalls, Niagara Falls, is located on the Niagara River at the border between western New York and Canada.

Among the state's many lakes are Lake Champlain, which New York shares with Vermont and Canada; Lake George, where several French and Indian War and Revolutionary War battles were fought; and the eleven slender lakes in the western half of the state which are called the *Finger Lakes.* The state has thousands of smaller lakes, including Lake Placid, which twice has been the site of the Winter Olympics.

In the southeast, where the Atlantic Ocean borders the state, New York has several famous islands. The only part of New York City that is attached to the mainland is the Bronx. The rest of the city is located on Manhattan Island, Staten Island, and Long Island. Besides the part that belongs to New York City, Long Island has dozens of other towns on it. In fact, more people live on Long Island (which is about 120 miles long) than live in about forty of the fifty states!

This beautiful state has had a fascinating history. Long ago, the Iroquois and other Indian tribes were New York's only inhabitants. The Dutch (people from The Netherlands) were the first Europeans to colonize the state. They introduced many Dutch customs and foods that are still part of American life, including dough-nuts and the Santa Claus tradition. Later the

English seized New York and made it one of their thirteen colonies, along with Virginia, Massachusetts, New Hampshire, Connecticut, Maryland, Rhode Island, Delaware, Pennsylvania, North Carolina, New Jersey, South Carolina, and Georgia.

After living under British rule for many years, people in New York and the other colonies fought the Revolutionary War (1775–1783) to free themselves from England, the mother country. Nearly one-third of all Revolutionary War battles were fought in New York State, including the pivotal Battle of Saratoga. George Washington spent a great deal of time in New York directing the American war efforts there. Shortly after the Americans won the Revolutionary War, New York City served as the capital of the United States for more than five years. George Washington, the country's first president, was inaugurated in New York City and lived in a house at a spot where the Brooklyn Bridge now stands.

Washington is thought to have given New York its nickname, the Empire State, when he predicted that the state would one day become the center of the American empire. New York lived up to his expectations. By 1850 it was the nation's leading state in both population and manufacturing, and today it is second only to California in both those categories. Besides the books and magazines already mentioned, New York products include cameras and film, clocks, surgical instruments, computers, and clothes. Nearly everyone in the United States comes into contact with some New York products every day.

The Empire State has also produced many famous people. Presidents Martin Van Buren, Millard Fillmore, Theodore Roosevelt, and Franklin Delano Roosevelt were born in New York State. Alexander Hamilton, who performed many services for the United States in its early years, was not born in New York, but he lived most of his life there. Authors Herman Melville, James Fenimore Cooper, Washington Irving, James Baldwin, and Maurice Sendak hailed from the Empire State, too. So did baseball players Lou Gehrig and Sandy Koufax and basketball player Kareem Abdul-Jabbar. Jonas Salk, the doctor who conquered polio, and Shirley Chisholm, the first black woman to serve in our country's Congress, were also born in New York.

But before these people could make their marks on American history, the colonists had to settle and build New York. And before the colonists arrived, New York's history was shaped by—the Indians.

11

Herman Melville

Kareem Abdul-Jabbar

Jonas Salk

Shirley Chisholm

Idyllic view of Manhattan Island in the sixteenth century

Chapter II

The Indians of New York

The natives [the Indians] are a very good people, for when they saw that I would not remain, they supposed that I was afraid of their bows, and taking the arrows they broke them in pieces and threw them into the fire.

> *Henry Hudson describing Indians he met while exploring New York in 1609*

Little is known about the Indians who first lived in what is now New York State more than 11,000 years ago. We know that these early people survived mainly by hunting deer and other animals. Some of their stone spear points and tools have been found.

By the year 1300, two families of modern Indians lived in New York. One group, the Algonquians, lived in what is now the south-eastern part of the state. The other group, the more powerful Iroquois, dominated the rest of New York.

The Iroquois were divided into five tribes that shared similar languages and life-styles. The five tribes were the Mohawk, the Oneida, the

Artist's concept of an Indian village of longhouses in New York, prior to Dutch occupation

Onondaga, the Cayuga, and the Seneca. Although other Indians and the Europeans who arrived later called these Indians the Iroquois, they called themselves the *Hodenosaunee*, meaning "People of the Longhouse."

They gave themselves this name because they lived in large dwellings called longhouses. A typical longhouse was about a hundred feet long and twenty-five feet wide. Built of logs and bark, longhouses resembled large barns. A typical Iroquois village had about ten longhouses, each with about eight families living in it. The Iroquois generally built their villages on hilltops and surrounded them with high wooden fences called palisades.

Within the longhouse each family had its own living space, screened off by animal skins. Along the walls and about one foot off the floor were wooden platforms on which the family slept. Since they had no tables or chairs, the family also ate their meals on their sleeping platforms. Beneath the platforms, and on small wooden shelves high up on the walls, the family stored clothes, tools, clay cooking pots and bowls, and food supplies.

The Iroquois obtained most of their food by hunting, fishing, and farming. As was generally the case with the American Indians, the women did the farming. Corn, beans, and squash—called the "three sisters"—were the main crops. The women also grew tobacco and sunflowers (for their seeds).

The men hunted with bows and arrows, clubs, and spears. Hunting parties went out for as long as several months and traveled as far as Ohio or Canada. Among the animals the men brought home were deer, elk, moose, bears, and wild turkeys. The men also paddled their canoes along New York's rivers and lakes, where they fished with bone hooks and nets.

Except during festivals, the Indians ate one meal a day, at about noon. The women did much of their cooking inside the longhouse, especially when the weather was cold. A longhouse had no chimney or windows. But some of the smoke escaped through openings in the roof.

The women used corn, the most important Iroquois food, to make soups, breads, puddings, and other dishes. They prepared tasty stews by mixing vegetables with meat. Much like some cooks do today, the women poured sunflower oil into their pots to keep them from burning.

The women also had the job of collecting maple sap in the early spring. After it was collected, it was boiled until it thickened into maple syrup. The Iroquois loved maple syrup. They poured it over cornmeal cakes, made it into maple sugar candy, and put it on popcorn to make a treat called "snow food." They also mixed maple syrup with strawberries, blueberries, and other berries to make fruit drinks.

Plants provided much more than food. Corn yielded dozens of household items. Children folded cornhusks into dolls. Women braided cornhusks to make floor mats, bedding, clothes-lines, and baby hammocks. Corncobs were turned into back scratchers and pipes for smoking. Corn kernels were strung together into pretty necklaces. And corn pulp was used to dye skins.

Corn even provided medical supplies. An ointment made from crushed cornstalks was applied to wounds. The injuries were then covered with cornhusk bandages. Medicines were made out of berries, bark, and roots. For example, tea made from the twigs of the serviceberry bush was given to people with stomach problems.

Animals provided household items too. Clothes and moccasins were made out of deerskins. Bear skins made good blankets. Small bones were turned into needles and fishing hooks. Turtle claws became arrow tips. Deer shoulder bones were converted into hoes.

Beaded moccasins, Mohawk

Although fifty people often lived in one longhouse, they rarely fought or argued. Most of the people in a longhouse were related, and each person knew what was expected of him or her.

The mothers were the heads of the Iroquois families. When a woman and man married, they went to live in the longhouse of her extended family. In addition to doing all the farming and housework, the wife did most of the child raising. The women also chose the chiefs and told them what to discuss at important meetings. The oldest woman in the longhouse was generally considered the head of the dwelling, and settled any serious arguments that occurred.

While the women were considered the brains of the family, the men provided most of the muscle. They cleared trees to make room for villages, built the longhouses, hunted, fished, and made tools.

Pipe tomahawks, Iroquois

17

Baby carrier, Mohawk

Iroquois men were also regarded as the fiercest Indian warriors north of Mexico.

Iroquois children received a great deal of love and attention. Babies were wrapped in moss diapers and carried on their mothers' backs in cradle boards. While a mother worked, the cradle board was hung from a tree branch. Children who misbehaved were never spanked. Instead, a naughty child received a dipperful of water in the face or a ducking in a cold stream. An older child who misbehaved might be temporarily banished by his grandmother from the longhouse.

There were no schools for the young Iroquois. Instead, children learned by observing and working alongside their elders. Little boys and girls helped their mothers with the housework and farming. Girls continued to work alongside their mothers as they got older. But by the age of eight, boys entered the company of older males, who taught them how to hunt and fight.

Iroquois children learned their people's beliefs from stories told by the tribal elders. On cold winter nights the people of the longhouse listened as the storyteller explained how the world was created, how the chipmunk got its stripes, or how the first people outwitted the Flying Heads and other evil spirits.

At the beginning of time [began the Iroquois creation story] the ancestors of people lived in the sky. One day a giant tree was uprooted in the sky world. The sky chief's daughter tumbled through the hole but managed to grab a handful of seeds from the giant tree as she fell. The sky princess finally reached the water world, where she began to drown. Duck and Swan tried to save the princess, but she was too heavy for them. Finally, Turtle swam up from the depths of the water world and took the princess on his back. So that the princess would have earth to live on, Muskrat dived to the bottom of the water world and brought up a speck of magic earth. The earth grew and grew until it became our world. The sky princess dropped her seeds onto the earth, and that was how life on our world began.

As the elder told a story, the people would say "Hah! Hah!" at regular intervals. This showed that they were paying attention. The Iroquois had no written language. Therefore the young had to memorize the stories so that one day they could tell them to the next generation.

The Iroquois believed that the world was home to many good and evil spirits. To give thanks to the good ones, they held six yearly festivals. First came the New Year Festival which took place about February 1. Then came the Maple Festival, the Corn Planting Festival, the Strawberry Festival, and the Green Corn Festival. In the fall, when most of the crops were gathered, the Iroquois held their Harvest Festival.

Lacrosse was often a dangerous game.

During their festivals the Indians offered prayers of thanksgiving to their gods. For example, at the Maple Festival they thanked the forest spirits for providing maple sap. They burned tobacco leaves while they prayed, because they believed that the smoke carried their prayers up to the gods. Food was another important part of the festivals. During the Strawberry Festival, for example, the Iroquois ate crushed strawberries topped with maple syrup.

Sports were played at festival time, too. Lacrosse—a game in which two teams use sticks to try to hit a ball into each other's goal—was their favorite. The Iroquois did not play with ten or twelve players, as is done today. Instead, lacrosse matches often pitted one village against another, with each team fielding more than one hundred players. The game was extremely violent, because players often deliberately hit each other with the sticks.

In another Iroquois game the contestants tried to hurl their spears through rolling hoops. The Iroquois also enjoyed foot races, arrow-shooting contests, and a dice game played with cherry stones.

Village life was sometimes interrupted by war. For several hundred years after they arrived in New York in about 1300, the five Iroquois tribes made war on each other. They fought over boundaries and over fishing and hunting rights. Finally, perhaps not long after Columbus first arrived in America, the five Iroquois tribes made a peace treaty. A Mohawk Indian named Hiawatha was largely responsible for persuading the five tribes to stop fighting and form a union. Called the League of the Five Nations, this federation was one of North America's most powerful Indian organizations between the 1500s and the late 1700s.

The League of the Five Nations created a council consisting of about fifty chiefs, who were chosen by the women of the five tribes. Each year, the

In 1724, a French writer illustrated his account of the League of Five Nations and the wampum belt which recorded the "laws" of the Five Nations.

Tribal symbol of the Five Nations

council met at a village near Onondaga Lake and present-day Syracuse, New York. As the chiefs sat around the council fire, they settled boundary disputes between the Five Nations. The council also had to give its approval if one of the tribes wanted to go to war.

Like other North American Indians, the Iroquois believed that the surprise raid was the best way to wage a war. The Europeans who arrived during the 1600s considered the raid a "sneaky" way to fight, but the Indians however, thought it was the height of stupidity to march out and fight in the open as the Europeans did.

Once war was declared, the Iroquois' goal was to kill the enemy with minimal risk to their own warriors.

Iroquois war parties walked along trails (some of which now have highways built directly over them) or paddled down rivers in canoes. When they neared the enemy village—usually an Algonquian one—they waited. Suddenly, in the dead of night, the Iroquois would burst in upon their sleeping enemies.

The second group of Indians, the Algonquians, probably arrived in what is now New York in about 1000 A.D. They most likely lived and hunted over a large portion of the area early on, but about 1300 A.D. the Iroquois arrived and drove the Algonquians into southeastern New York. Among the Algonquian tribes that lived in New York were

Seth Eastman's account of a battle between Dakota and Algonquian Indians

the Delaware, Wappinger, Mahican, Munsee, and Montauk.

The New York Algonquian tribes farmed, hunted, and fished much like the Iroquois. Also like the Iroquois, they worshipped numerous gods. Some of them lived in longhouses like those of the Iroquois, but many others lived in bark-covered huts called wigwams.

By 1600 the Algonquian Indians of New York and other areas of the Northeast had developed wampum—polished shell beads strung together on belts. Some of the wampum belts were used as money. Some had bead pictures on them that conveyed messages from one person or tribe to another. Some contained pictures that recorded tribal history. The Iroquois did not make wampum of their own. They obtained it by trading for it and stealing it from the Algonquians.

Although the Algonquians were as brave and intelligent as the Iroquois, they could not match them in battle. The Algonquians were less organized than the Iroquois, and they did not cooperate with each other as much as the People of the Longhouse did. But neither the Iroquois nor the Algonquians were a match for the people who reached New York in the early 1600s—the strangers from across the ocean.

HIAWATHA (1525?–1575?)

In 1855 Henry Wadsworth Longfellow published a narrative poem called *The Song of Hiawatha*. Longfellow used the name Hiawatha in his famous poem because he liked the sound of it. Although Longfellow's poem is not historically accurate, its subject is partly based on a real Hiawatha, who was a Mohawk chief and one of the founders of the League of the Five Nations.

Hiawatha probably grew up in or near what is now New York State in the early 1500s, although some sources say that he lived as early as the 1400s. According to some stories, Hiawatha's wife and seven daughters were killed by Ododarhoh, a man so evil it was believed that snakes grew out of his head.

After the death of his wife and daughters, Hiawatha spoke to no one and took no part in his tribe's activities. Then one day he met a man named Degandawida, who was preaching that the Iroquois should stop fighting each other and join together to form an empire. Unfortunately, Degandawida stuttered and could not get his ideas across to others. Hiawatha, on the other hand, had been a fine speaker before he had become a hermit. Hiawatha agreed to travel with Degandawida and explain his idea of an Iroquois empire.

Hiawatha convinced all but the Onondaga tribes to form a federation. Then he went to the Onondaga leader, Ododarhoh, the wicked man who had killed his family. When Ododarhoh saw that Hiawatha had overcome his hatred and had come to him in peace, he abandoned his evil ways and led his people into the federation. It was said that Hiawatha combed the snakes out of Ododarhoh's head. In fact, it is sometimes said that the name Hiawatha means "He Who Combs."

When Europeans arrived in New York, they heard stories about Hiawatha that had been handed down for generations. These stories varied, but they all agreed that Hiawatha and Degandawida had been responsible for forming the League of the Five Nations. What became of Hiawatha after he helped found the League is not known.

Henry Hudson and crew members trading with Indians on the
Hudson River

Chapter III

Exploration and Early Dutch Colonization

The land is good and fruitful in everything.

> *Early Dutch colonist describing New York during the 1640s*

For hundreds of years, the Indians had what is now known as New York to themselves. Then in the early 1500s, strangers arrived by ship. At first they just studied the land from a distance. Giovanni da Verrazano (1485?–1528), an Italian working for France, may have been the first explorer to reach the area. In the spring of 1524, he probably sailed his ship, the *Dauphine*, into lower New York Bay and anchored the craft near present-day Verrazano-Narrows Bridge. Verrazano and his men may have also landed on Staten Island, which is now part of New York City.

Giovanni da Verrazano

Later in the century, the Spanish and the French explored what is today New York State. The French may have built several small forts, where they traded for furs with the Indians. But

27

no permanent colonies were built during the 1500s.

By the early 1600s, the French were starting to take control of Canada. In 1609 the Frenchman Samuel de Champlain (1567?–1635) came down from Quebec, Canada, with some Algonquian Indians. Champlain explored a large lake at the place where New York, Vermont, and Canada meet. He named this body of water Lake Champlain after himself.

Samuel de Champlain

The Indians guided Samuel de Champlain into northeastern New York with the understanding that he would help them fight the Iroquois. Near what is now Ticonderoga, New York, Champlain and two of his men, together with a party of Algonquians, encountered a group of Iroquois. Champlain carried a strange stick that the Iroquois had never seen before. The Iroquois approached, ready to attack. Suddenly, something exploded out of the stick Champlain carried. Two Iroquois chiefs fell dead, and a third was fatally wounded. The Algonquians, who had been losing to the Iroquois for three centuries, were very happy. But due to this and other encounters, the Iroquois and the French became enemies.

The French were more interested in building fur-trading posts than in founding settlements.

Therefore, they sent no colonists to New York following Champlain's exploration. But soon people who were interested in colonization came to New York. These were the Dutch, the people of The Netherlands.

In 1609, the same year that Champlain explored New York for France, the Dutch sent Henry Hudson to find a shorter route to Asia. With about twenty men, Hudson set sail from The Netherlands in a ship called *Halve Maen*, which is Dutch for *Half Moon*. It was the spring of 1609, and Hudson and his men were not thinking about the New York region when they left The Netherlands. In fact, they first headed northeast in hope of finding a passage through the Barents Sea to Asia.

Henry Hudson

The *Half Moon* encountered ice and bad weather in the Barents Sea, however, and had to turn back. Not finding a new eastern route to Asia, Hudson decided to search for a western route. Instead of returning to The Netherlands, he traveled west across the Atlantic Ocean toward America.

In summer of 1609 the *Half Moon* reached the coast of Newfoundland, Canada. The ship sailed down the coast of Canada, then continued down the East Coast of the present-day United States.

Hudson and his men sailed past Maine, New Hampshire, Massachusetts, Rhode Island, Connecticut, New York, New Jersey, Delaware, Maryland, Virginia, and North Carolina. The *Half Moon* went as far as Cape Hatteras along the North Carolina coast, then Hudson turned back northward to more thoroughly explore several places that had been passed.

Hudson briefly explored Chesapeake Bay, the arm of the Atlantic Ocean that extends up along the Virginia coast and then divides Maryland into two parts. The explorer did not want to stay long in the Chesapeake Bay region, though, because it was English territory. Two years earlier, in 1607, the English had built their first permanent American settlement near Chesapeake Bay at Jamestown, Virginia. Hudson then explored Delaware Bay, the arm of the Atlantic separating Delaware from New Jersey. Later, in early September of 1609, the *Half Moon* entered New York Bay.

The Indians were excited by the arrival of the ship. They paddled out to meet her crew. In exchange for knives and beads, the Indians traded furs and tobacco. Thinking that the Indians would remain friendly, Hudson sent out a five-man party to explore the area that is now New

Indians paddling out to meet the crew of the *Half Moon*

York City. The men were returning to the *Half Moon* when two canoeloads of Indians suddenly attacked. One sailor was shot through the throat with an arrow and died, and two others were wounded.

Hudson then continued his search for a waterway through America to Asia. He saw that a river stretched northward from the upper part of New York Bay. Hoping it would turn westward and cross America, Hudson sailed up this river. Later it was named the Hudson in his honor.

The *Half Moon* sailed up the Hudson River as far north as present-day Albany. Disappointed at not finding the fabled waterway to Asia (no such natural waterway across the United States exists), Hudson turned the *Half Moon* around and sailed back down the river. He stopped occasionally to trade with friendly Indians. Then he and his men returned to The Netherlands.

Although they were disappointed that Hudson had not found the water route to Asia, the Dutch realized that New York could make them wealthy. The Indians there were eager to trade valuable furs for tools, weapons, and cloth. New York also had great farmland that would be valuable if the Dutch ever wanted to set up a colony there.

During the next several years the Dutch sent other expeditions to New York to explore the area and to trade with the Indians. In 1613, the Dutch explorer Adriaen Block arrived in a small ship called the *Tiger*. After trading for furs with the Indians along the Hudson River, Block anchored off an island the Indians called *Man-a-hat-ta* (Island of the Hills). This island is now called Manhattan and is part of New York City.

While anchored off the tip of Manhattan where Battery Park now stands, the *Tiger* caught fire. Captain Block and his men swam to Manhattan

Captain Block and his men building the *Onrust*

Island, but the ship was completely destroyed. Winter was coming, and the men had no way to get home and no place to live.

With the help of friendly Indians, Block and his men built cabins that resembled the Indians' wigwams. There they passed the winter of 1613-14. The crew of the *Tiger* are generally considered to be the first non-Indians to live in what is now New York City.

In the spring of 1614, Block and his men cut down timber on Manhattan Island and used it to build a new ship, which they named the *Onrust.*

The *Onrust*, which means "Restless," was too small to cross the Atlantic Ocean, but Captain Block used it to explore regions near New York. He sailed up the Connecticut River, claiming Connecticut for The Netherlands. He explored the Rhode Island region, and he may have been the person who gave it its name. Finally, Block met a larger ship that took him and his men back to The Netherlands.

Based on the explorations of Hudson, Block, and others, The Netherlands claimed a large area of what is now the United States. This region included parts of the present states of New York, New Jersey, Connecticut, and Delaware. They called this territory New Netherland. New York was the largest and most important part of New Netherland.

The Dutch built trading posts in New York, including one built in 1614 near where Albany now stands. Several years later, the Dutch began to colonize New York.

In 1621 some wealthy businessmen in The Netherlands formed a company called the Dutch West India Company. The government of The Netherlands gave this company the right to build settlements and trade with the Indians in New Netherland. In fact, no one but the Dutch West

The West India House
in Amsterdam

India Company was allowed to trade in the area.

In 1624 the Dutch West India Company sent about thirty families, consisting of 110 men, women, and children, to New Netherland. They sailed in a large ship called the *New Netherland*. After two months at sea, the *New Netherland* reached the mouth of the Hudson River in the spring of 1624. There the people scattered. About eighteen of the families continued up the Hudson River and founded a settlement called Fort Orange, which is now Albany. Fort Orange was the first permanent non-Indian settlement built in what is now New York State. Other people settled in Connecticut, New Jersey, and Delaware, and a handful colonized Manhattan Island.

More Dutch colonists brought their cattle, horses, and other livestock, to Manhattan Island in 1625. That year, the colonists built Fort Amsterdam and began laying out a town on Manhattan Island. They named the town New Amsterdam after the city of Amsterdam in The Netherlands. It eventually grew into New York City.

> *Since the Dutch had other names for what we call New York State and New York City, here is a short review. The Dutch founded New Amsterdam (now New York City) in 1625. New Amsterdam became the chief town in the Dutch colony of New Netherland, which comprised parts of what are now New York State, New Jersey, Connecticut, and Delaware.*

Another group of colonists sent by the Dutch West India Company arrived in New Amsterdam in May of 1626. The handful of people who had already settled in New Amsterdam excitedly greeted these newcomers for among them was the colony's new governor, Peter Minuit.

Minuit wanted to make sure that there would be no trouble with the Indians over the ownership of Manhattan Island, the site of New Amsterdam. Before doing anything else, Minuit met with some Indians who were in the area and offered to buy Manhattan Island from them. The Indians accepted cloth, knives, beads, and trinkets worth

Peter Minuit

Governor Minuit
purchasing
Manhattan Island
from the Indians

about sixty Dutch guilders (about $24) for Manhattan Island.* Today, you could spend nearly that much just parking the family car in the city for a few hours!

One dollar for every square mile isn't much, so it sounds as though the Indians did not make a very good deal. But it appears that the Indians who sold Manhattan to the Dutch may have just been passing through at the time. In that case they had no claim to the land and no right to sell it.

* A copy of a letter announcing the purchase of Manhattan appears on page 146

Governor Minuit also supervised the building of houses, streets, and public buildings in New Amsterdam. He also oversaw construction of *bouweries* (Dutch for farms). The town grew slowly at first, partly because very few Dutch people wanted to come to America. During the 1600s, The Netherlands was enjoying its "Golden Age." The country at that time had the highest standard of living of any nation. The Netherlands also had more religious tolerance than any other European nation. The Pilgrims who fled England because of religious persecution lived in The Netherlands for a dozen years before sailing to Massachusetts. People generally wanted to go to The Netherlands, not leave it.

Nonetheless, there were some Dutch people who thought they could become rich in the new country or who simply wanted to start a new life in America. During the 1620s and 1630s, some of these people sailed to New Amsterdam. By 1640 the town's population was about five hundred. The Dutch settlers slowly fanned out from New Amsterdam and founded other new towns. Sometimes they named them after cities in The Netherlands. Two of these were Breuckelen, now Brooklyn, and New Haarlem, which is the section of New York City called Harlem. New York City is

The town of New Amsterdam grew rapidly.

composed of many little towns that were independent of each other in colonial days.

The Dutch West India Company wanted more people to farm and trade in New Netherland so that the colony would produce more money. To encourage settlement, the company made a generous offer to its stockholders. Any stockholder who paid for fifty people to move to New Netherland would be rewarded with a large piece of land. The landowner would be called a *patroon* and would rule over the land and the people he had brought there, much as a king would rule.

The Dutch West India Company tried to settle what are now New York, New Jersey, Delaware, and Connecticut through the patroon system. But the system failed, partly because people did not want to be ruled by someone with absolute power. Only five patroonships were granted, and just one succeeded. The successful one, Rensselaerswyck, was named after the patroon Kiliaen Van Rensselaer, a diamond merchant. Van Rensselaer sent dozens of people to Rensselaerswyck, which occupied much of what are now Albany, Columbia, and Rensselaer counties in New York. Part of Rensselaerswyck became the present-day city of Rensselaer.

Because the Dutch were open about allowing minorities to settle in New Netherland, the colony soon became a melting pot for people of various nationalities and religions. Kiliaen Van Rensselaer, who never came to New Netherland, sent not only Dutch but also Norwegian, Danish, German, English, and Scottish people to Rensselaerswyck. Many English people were allowed to settle on what is now Long Island. Among them was the Englishwoman Lady Deborah Moody. In 1643 she bought land from the Indians and built a settlement that included the famous Coney Island at the southern tip of

Those who arrived in New Netherland brought what they thought they would need for a new life.

Brooklyn. The part of New York City called the Bronx was first settled by a Danish man named Jonas Bronck.

New Amsterdam had the greatest variety of people of any of the New Netherland towns. A French priest who visited New Amsterdam during the early 1640s reported that eighteen different languages were spoken in the town. By that time New Amsterdam had churches, numerous shops and taverns, and a few farms. The land where the United Nations headquarters now stands was a tobacco plantation when the Dutch ruled New Amsterdam.

Although they had at first liked the colonists, the Indians soon realized that the Swannekens ("the people from the salt sea") wanted more and more land. The Indians also knew that the colonists were sometimes willing to cheat them to get it. In 1638 the Dutch West India Company made relations with the Indians worse when they sent William Kieft to govern the colony. Almost single-handedly he destroyed whatever friendship remained between the Indians and the colonists.

Kieft decided that the best way to raise money to defend the colony was to tax the Indians. The native Americans had helped Adriaen Block and his crew survive the winter on Manhattan Island. They had provided land for the Dutch settlers and had taught them how to plant corn. It seemed unfair to them that they should now have to pay taxes to the Dutch.

Kieft, who wanted a fight with the Indians, then wrongly accused some Raritan Indians on Staten Island of stealing pigs. Soldiers sent to Staten Island by Governor Kieft killed several Indians, tortured others, and destroyed the Raritans' crops. The Indians struck back by killing four Staten Island farmers and burning some farms. Kieft then offered a reward for the head of any Raritan Indian.

Another event added fuel to the fire. In the summer of 1641, an Indian came to the house of a man named Claes Smit, who lived near New Amsterdam. The Indian asked for cloth in exchange for beaver skins. As Smit bent down to get the cloth, the Indian killed him with an ax.

Kieft learned where the Indian was hiding and asked his chief to turn him over to the Dutch. The chief refused, explaining that when the murderer was about twelve years old, he had seen his uncle murdered by some Dutch workmen. According to the Indian custom of blood revenge, the Indian had to kill a Dutchman to even the score. He had fulfilled that obligation—fifteen years later.

The governor decided to take vengeance on the Indians so they would not murder again. In early 1643 hundreds of Algonquian Indians were camped on Manhattan Island and also across the Hudson River in the area of what is now Jersey City, New Jersey. On the night of February 25, 1643, Governor William Kieft sent two groups of Fort Amsterdam soldiers to slaughter the camping Indians. The group sent to New Jersey murdered about eighty Indian men, women, and children. The soldiers threw Indian infants into the river and laughed as the children drowned. The group that marched to the Indian camp on

Manhattan killed forty of the Native Americans. When the soldiers returned to the fort, Kieft gave them medals.

At least eleven separate Algonquian tribes took to the warpath because of these massacres. During the next several years, they attacked and killed farm families in what are now New York, New Jersey, and Connecticut. Among those killed in the New York area was Anne Hutchinson (1591–1643), a religious leader who had helped found Portsmouth, Rhode Island. The situation in New Amsterdam became so dangerous that the settlers had to hide in the fort for safety.

Kieft asked The Netherlands for help, but Dutch officials would not send it. Instead they blamed the governor for what they called Kieft's Indian War. Finally, Kieft hired an English soldier named Captain John Underhill to attack the Indians.

Captain Underhill and an army of Dutch and English soldiers attacked and killed about 120 Canarsie Indians on Long Island. At about the same time, Dutch forces killed five hundred more Indians in what is now Westchester County. After losing hundreds of men, women, and children in a short time, the Algonquian Indians agreed to a peace treaty ending Kieft's Indian War in 1645.

Indians and citizens of New Amsterdam smoked the Pipe of Peace at the end of Kieft's War.

Kieft was despised not only by the Indians but also by most of the colonists. They opposed his taxes and strict laws. An outspoken New Amsterdam minister named Everardus Bogardus became one of Kieft's chief enemies. Bogardus gave sermons in which he compared the governor to a "monster," a "robber," and a "fountain of evil." In turn, the governor ordered his soldiers to play their drums outside the church during services.

Because of Reverend Bogardus and Kieft's many other enemies, the governor was recalled to The Netherlands in 1647. The Dutch West India Company selected a much more able man, Peter Stuyvesant, as the new governor.

HENRY HUDSON (?-1611)

Little is known about explorer Henry Hudson until 1607 when he made four famous voyages. He is believed to have been born in England and to have worked as a sailor in his early years.

During the early 1600s, merchants made fortunes by trading for spices, silks, and other treasures in Asia. But to reach Asia, they had to either sail around Africa's southern tip or make a difficult trip across Europe. It was widely believed that somewhere in the far northern part of the world there was a water route leading to Asia. Many people even thought that there was a warm open sea near the North Pole and that a ship could sail over it to Asia. In 1607 an English trading firm called the Muscovy Company hired Hudson to sail over the pole to Asia. In the spring of 1607, Henry Hudson, his young son John, and a ten-man crew left England in search of the short polar route to Asia. But their ship, the *Hopewell*, was blocked by ice a long way from the pole. In the summer of 1607, the expedition returned to England.

Having learned that it was impossible to reach Asia by sailing north over the pole, the Muscovy Company then hired Hudson to search for a northeastern route to Asia. In the spring of 1608, Hudson and his son John left England in the *Hopewell* and headed northeast. This second voyage also ended in failure because of ice. In fact, only Hudson's expert seamanship saved the *Hopewell* from being crushed by icebergs.

After twice failing to find the shortcut, Henry Hudson lost the support of the English trading company. But the Dutch East India Company of The Netherlands also believed that there was an ice-free route to Asia. Since Hudson knew these waters, the Dutch company hired him in 1609 to sail the *Half Moon* to the northeast. Blocked once more by ice, Hudson decided to head west. In the summer and fall of 1609, he and his son John explored much of America's east coast, including New York.

Although Hudson was disappointed at not finding the shortcut to Asia, this voyage later proved successful because it led to Dutch colonization of New Netherland. Hudson wanted one more chance to search for the shortcut for the Dutch East India Company, but the English government would not allow him to continue sailing for the Dutch. The English felt that Hudson was close to finding the northwest shortcut to Asia, and they wanted him to make the discovery while working for them.

The English provided Hudson with an excellent ship, the *Discovery*, and a crew of about two dozen men. Free to choose his own course, Hudson and his son John left England in the spring of 1610 and headed west toward Canada. He and his men explored what were later named the Hudson Strait and Hudson Bay in Canada. But in November, ice in the bay froze the *Discovery* in near the shoreline. The men spent the winter of 1610–11 cold, hungry, and sick on board their ship. Food became so scarce that they had to eat frogs and moss.

By early summer of 1611, the ice had broken and the *Discovery* was ready to head home. But the great explorer never reached his destination. Several crewmen who blamed Hudson for their near-starvation set him adrift in a small boat. John Hudson, several sick sailors, and others who were loyal to their captain, were also set adrift. The *Discovery* set out for home, leaving Hudson and the eight other behind in the tiny boat.

Not a trace was ever found of Henry and John Hudson and the seven other sailors. Several of the sailors who had taken part in the rebellion were tried for mutiny when they reached England, but they were later released from the charges.

PETER MINUIT (1580–1638)

Peter Minuit was born in what is now Germany, but as a young man he moved across the border into The Netherlands. Not much is known about Minuit's life, either in Europe or in America. It is known, however, that he played a major role in the early days of what are now New York and Delaware.

In 1625 the Dutch West India Company appointed Minuit governor of New Netherland. Shortly after arriving in the *Little Gull* in May of 1626, Minuit purchased Manhattan Island from the Indians and took the first steps toward building New Amsterdam (now New York City) into a thriving town.

Although Peter Minuit did a great deal to help New Netherland grow, officials in The Netherlands thought he granted too much land to the wealthy patroons. In 1631 he found himself, to use a Dutch expression, "kicked out onto the dike," or fired, as governor of New Netherland.

The Swedish, meanwhile, were also planning to set up a colony in America. Since Minuit was experienced in ruling a colony, the Swedish hired him to command their first expedition to America. In 1638 Minuit led the Swedish expedition up the Delaware River. At the site of what is now the city of Wilmington, they purchased land from the Indians and built Fort Christina, Delaware's first permanent non-Indian settlement. Shortly after founding Fort Christina, Peter Minuit sailed away on a trading expedition. On this trip the man who had helped settle both New York and Delaware was drowned in a hurricane. Governor Peter Stuyvesant captured Delaware for the Dutch in 1655 and made it part of the New Netherland Colony.

Stuyvesant's signature and his official seal

Governor Stuyvesant speaking before some townspeople

Chapter IV

Peter Stuyvesant Rules New Netherland

I shall rule you as a father his children.

*Peter Stuyvesant, soon after arriving in
New Amsterdam in the spring of 1647*

On May 11, 1647, the people of New Amsterdam
gathered at the docks, as they always did when
ships arrived. On this spring day the people
watched their new governor, Peter Stuyvesant,
climb down the rope ladder of the *Princess*. He
then boarded a smaller boat that brought him
ashore. As Stuyvesant stepped onto the dock on
his one real leg and one wooden one, soldiers in
the fort fired cannons to salute him.

Peter Stuyvesant had lost his leg while serving
as governor of some Dutch islands in the
Caribbean Sea. Because he wore a wooden leg
with silver bands around it, people called him
"Peg Leg Pete" or "Old Silver Leg" behind his
back. He also had another nickname—"Stubborn
Pete."

A drawing of New Amsterdam, published in 1656

Governor Stuyvesant was upset at what he found in New Amsterdam. The town had deteriorated under Kieft's rule. The fort was run-down and so were many of the houses in which the town's seven hundred people lived. People threw their garbage onto the dirt streets, relying on the livestock that roamed the town to serve as "garbagemen." Stuyvesant was also disturbed to find that many of the townspeople were drunkards. According to some estimates, in the early 1640s one out of every four New Amsterdam buildings was a liquor store or tavern. Drunken brawls and knife fights were common, and tipsy men drove their wagons and carts recklessly through the streets.

50

As governor, Stuyvesant helped solve many of New Amsterdam's problems. He ordered taverns closed at nine o'clock at night, and he imposed stiff penalties on those who brawled and fought with knives. He made it safer to walk through New Amsterdam by ordering drivers to get out of their wagons and lead their horses through town. The only street where drivers could still ride in their wagons was the wide one that is now called Broadway, but even there they had to obey a low speed limit.

Some of Stuyvesant's most important measures protected the town from fire, which was a great hazard during colonial times. One spark from a poorly made chimney could set the town ablaze within seconds. Less than a year after the English built their first permanent American settlement at Jamestown, Virginia, a fire destroyed much of it. The Pilgrim colony at Plymouth, Massachusetts, and many other colonial towns were also destroyed or badly damaged by fire.

Stuyvesant helped formulate a fire code requiring people to keep their chimneys clean and their homes as fireproof as possible. He appointed four wardens to enforce the code and fine violators. The money collected from fines went toward the purchase of fire buckets.

Whenever a fire was spotted, people rushed from their homes with their fire buckets and formed two lines called "bucket brigades." One brigade dumped water onto the flames while the other passed the empty buckets to the well, where they were refilled.

"Old Silver Leg" also organized the colony's first police force, the "rattle watch." This force consisted of nine men who patrolled the streets between tavern closing time and six o'clock in the morning. Each rattle watchman wore an orange and blue uniform and carried a lantern, sword, musket, pistol, and large rattle. A watchman who spotted a lawbreaker would shake his rattle to attract help. If he spotted a fire, he would yell "*Brand!*" the Dutch word for fire. People who heard the cries quickly organized their bucket brigades.

The town improved in many other ways too. In Stuyvesant's time New Amsterdam was just a small fraction the size of modern New York City. Stuyvesant ordered a wall built across the northern edge of town to protect New Amsterdam from surprise attack. This wall was removed in about 1700, but the place where it stood is still known as Wall Street. During Stuyvesant's governorship, the town's first hospital and post

This sketch of Wall Street in 1653 was drawn from the original plans for the palisade (shown in the inset). On March 31, 1644, people were asked to help build the wall.

"Resolved . . . that a fence or park shall be made beginning at the Great Bouwery and extending to Emanuel's plantation, and every one . . . is warned to repair thither next Monday being the 4th of April at 7 o'clock . . . with tools and aid in constructing said fence . . . Let every one take notice hereof and communicate it to his neighbor."

office were built. Stuyvesant also ordered the fort repaired, directed the building of paved streets, arranged for garbage to be carted away instead of dumped in the streets, and controlled the number of pigs and other animals that roamed the town.

Despite all this, Stuyvesant was widely disliked. For one thing, all these improvements required higher taxes, which people resented. Stuyvesant was also a bossy, short-tempered man who had little regard for the opinions of others. He was even known to ignore the orders of his employer, the Dutch West India Company.

At the junction of Pearl and Chatham streets was the City Commons and a Jewish cemetery.

The company wanted minorities to be as welcome in New Netherland as they were in the homeland. Stuyvesant, however, was too prejudiced to accept certain people. In 1654 about thirty Jewish people arrived in New Amsterdam from Brazil. They were descendants of Jews who had been expelled from Spain by King Ferdinand and Queen Isabella in 1492, the year Columbus first came to America. Stuyvesant wrote a letter to the company asking that "none of the Jewish nation be permitted to infest New Netherland," but the company wouldn't let him evict the Jews.

Nonetheless, the handful of New Amsterdam Jews were not allowed to have a synagogue at first, and so they held their services secretly. The first Jewish Rosh Hashanah services in what is now the United States were held in a secret spot in New Amsterdam on September 12, 1654. This marked the beginning of Congregation Shearith Israel, which today is the oldest Jewish congregation in North America.

In 1657 another group that had been persecuted elsewhere arrived in New Amsterdam, only to find bigotry there too. These were the Quakers, or Society of Friends. The Quakers were, and still are, a peaceful people who hated war and emphasized inward spirituality. The Puritans of Massachusetts hated the Quakers and were very cruel to them. Many of the Quakers who came to New Amsterdam in 1657 had been expelled from Boston, the Massachusetts capital.

When two Quaker women began preaching in

Quaker women preached in the streets of New Amsterdam.

the streets of New Amsterdam, Stuyvesant jailed them for a time and later banished them from the colony. About the same time, a young Quaker named Robert Hodgson settled in Hempstead, just a few miles east of New Amsterdam on Long Island. After convincing several Long Islanders to become Quakers, Hodgson was arrested and sentenced to work at hard labor for two years.

Claiming that he had done nothing wrong, Hodgson refused to do the work. Stuyvesant then threw him into prison, with the approval of many Dutch ministers. The governor ordered the Quaker whipped every day with a tarred rope until he agreed to serve the punishment. Although they were a gentle people, the Quakers were mentally tough and willing to die for their beliefs. Hodgson would not give in, even when he was suspended from the ceiling by his wrists and lashed until he was nearly dead. The only thing that kept Stuyvesant from killing Hodgson was that the governor's own sister begged him to let the Quaker go. Hodgson was freed but was banished from New Netherland.

To protest the governor's cruelty, Quakers in Flushing (now part of New York City) held their services in the open instead of in secret as they had in the past. After Stuyvesant ordered several

A Quaker meeting house built in 1670 in Flushing

of them arrested, thirty-one English and Dutch people in the Flushing area wrote a letter of protest to the governor around Christmastime of 1657. In their letter, known as the Flushing Remonstrance, these brave people said that "love, peace, and liberty" should be extended to everyone. This was one of the first times that colonial Americans insisted that all people have certain basic rights.

When officials of the Dutch West India Company heard about Stuyvesant's cruelty toward the Quakers, they ordered him to mend his ways. Reluctantly, the governor stopped persecuting the Quakers, just as he had somewhat stopped persecuting the Jews.

While New Netherlanders were arguing among themselves about religion and taxes, they also faced problems with other nations. By the mid-1600s large numbers of English people had moved into New Netherland. When the powerful English demanded several large chunks of New Netherland, the Dutch had no choice but to comply. In 1650 Governor Stuyvesant agreed to a treaty that gave England control of almost all of Connecticut and a large portion of modern-day Long Island.

Sweden also posed a threat. In 1638 Swedes under Peter Minuit settled in Delaware. They

Governor Stuyvesant demanded that Swedish settlers, who were holding Fort Casimir, surrender.

named the Delaware region New Sweden, ignoring the fact that the Dutch considered it part of New Netherland. The Swedes weren't nearly as powerful as the English, however. In 1651 Governor Stuyvesant went to Delaware where he built Fort Casimir in an effort to wrest control of Delaware from the Swedes. In 1654 the Swedes captured Fort Casimir, but the next year Stuyvesant settled the issue by leading hundreds of soldiers on seven warships to Delaware, where they recaptured Fort Casimir. The Swedes then relinquished all of Delaware to the Dutch.

While Stuyvesant and his soldiers were capturing Delaware, trouble broke out at home between the colonists and the Indians. It started on a September day in 1655, when a young Indian girl entered an orchard near what is now the intersection of Broadway and Wall Street in New York City. The girl was picking a few peaches in the orchard when the orchard's owner, a former sheriff named Hendrick Van Dyck, spotted her and shot her dead. This started what is known as the Peach War.

At dawn of September 15, 1655, dozens of canoes carrying more than five hundred Indians approached New Amsterdam along the Hudson River. During the next three days, the Indians rampaged on both sides of the Hudson. The Indians killed about 100 colonists, took about 150 prisoners, destroyed Hoboken and Jersey City in New Jersey, and did great damage to New Amsterdam. The people of New Amsterdam had to crowd into the fort for safety as they had done during Kieft's Indian War.

When he returned to New Amsterdam from Delaware in October of 1655, Stuyvesant found much of his colony in ashes. In what was one of the best decisions of his governorship, he decided to not take revenge on the Indians. The governor made this decision because he felt the colonists had brought on the war themselves. Stuyvesant made peace with the Indians, won the release of a number of their prisoners, and rebuilt the damaged colony.

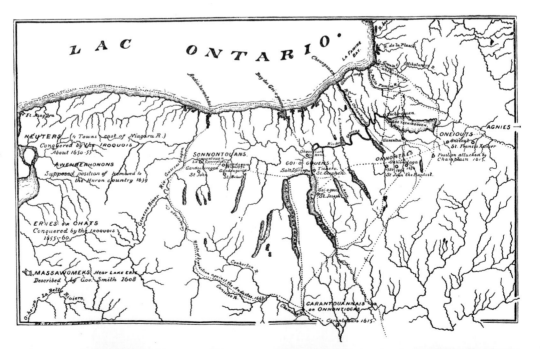

A map of the Five Iroquois Nations in the mid-sixteenth century drawn by John S. Clark in 1879

PETER STUYVESANT (1610?-1672)

Peter Stuyvesant was born the son of a minister in the northern part of The Netherlands. Peter was good at Latin and was very intelligent, but he did not have the temperament to become a minister like his father. What he did possess were great bravery, a sudden and fierce temper, and a strong desire to visit distant lands.

In 1635 Stuyvesant went to work for the Dutch West India Company. First the company sent him to Brazil, which the Dutch had partially conquered in 1630. He began as a clerk but later rose to the position of administrator of several Brazilian trading posts. Then in 1643 the company made him governor of Curaçao and other Dutch-controlled islands in the Caribbean Sea.

In 1644 Stuyvesant led Dutch soldiers on a raid against the Portuguese on the island of St. Martin, six hundred miles northeast of Curaçao. The attack failed, and Stuyvesant was so badly wounded that his right leg had to be amputated. He returned to The Netherlands for the attachment of an artificial leg. A year later, in 1645, he asked the Dutch West India Company for a new assignment.

Stuyvesant was named governor of New Netherland and arrived in New Amsterdam in spring of 1647. Many people disliked him from the start. They said he dressed and acted like a one-legged peacock and that he ruled them like the czar of Russia.

For nearly two decades, New Netherlanders struggled with "Stubborn Pete" to gain more control of their government. When people threatened to tell officials in The Netherlands about his refusal to share power, Stuyvesant said: "If anyone during my administration shall appeal, I will make him a foot shorter and send the pieces to Holland, and let him appeal in that way!" And yet in some ways, Stuyvesant was the savior of New Netherland. He brought law and order to the colony and, because he talked tough and was ready to back up his words, Stuyvesant even scared the Indians into avoiding fights with the Dutch.

But when the English arrived in their warships in summer of 1664, Stuyvesant couldn't outbluff them. Hopelessly outmanned and outgunned, and with few of his people willing to fight, Stuyvesant was forced to surrender. He spent several years in The Netherlands explaining why he had surrendered the land he had come to love. In 1667 he returned to New Amsterdam, where he spent his last years gardening and reading the Bible. Part of Peter Stuyvesant's farm is now the area called the Bowery in New York City.

A typical Dutch cottage on Beaver Street in 1679

Chapter V

Everyday Life in the Dutch Colony

Eigen haard is goud waard.

Dutch saying, meaning, "Your home and family are worth gold"

LIFE IN NEW AMSTERDAM

By 1660, about five thousand colonists lived in what is now New York State. The colony's largest town, New Amsterdam, had little more than a thousand people. New Amsterdam occupied only the southwestern tip of Manhattan Island.*

The people of New Amsterdam lived in tall, narrow, steep-roofed brick and wooden homes. Almost every front door had a large brass knocker shaped like a lion's or a dog's head. As was the custom in The Netherlands, many doors were divided into upper and lower halves. A person could talk to friends or relatives on the outside by opening the top half of the door, while the closed part kept pigs and chickens from wandering in off the streets.

* A map of Manhattan in 1661 appears on page 147

Furniture, much of it imported from The Netherlands, was heavy, sturdy, and simple. The Dutch were fond of stools and benches and often sat on them instead of on chairs. Because they often had to sleep in the living room, they found interesting ways to hide their beds. Some were built right into the walls. Sleeping in one of them must have been a little like sleeping in a big cupboard!

Dutch bed

A huge fireplace was an important part of a Dutch home. The Dutch decorated their fireplaces with tiles on which were painted scenes from Bible stories. While a family sat around the fireplace, the mother and father would explain the Bible passages that were illustrated on the tiles. The fireplace not only provided heat and light, it was also the place where food was cooked. Much of it was cooked in a big kettle suspended over the fire. Baked goods were prepared in an oven built into the chimney bricks alongside the fireplace.

The Dutch were hearty eaters and drinkers. Most families had vegetable gardens behind their houses, and some wealthy people owned large bouweries (farms) located beyond the town limits. The Indians taught the first colonists how to grow and prepare corn, pumpkins, and squash. Among the colonists' other food crops were apples, peaches, peas, carrots, cherries, plums, and

Not every New Amsterdam family was as well fed as the one pictured above

lettuce. In addition, many families raised cows, chickens, and pigs for food.

As the Indians had done for so many years, hunters and fishermen brought back deer, wild turkeys, ducks, geese, partridges, oysters, clams, lobsters, and crabs for the family dinner table. In those days New Amsterdam teemed with so much wildlife that a law had to be passed banning hunting within the town.

The Dutch introduced a number of dishes that are still popular today. They made a cabbage salad in vinegar that they called *koolsla*, which is now called cole slaw. They made fried cakes they called *olykoecks*, or doughnuts. The New Netherlanders also introduced small twisted cakes known as *crullers*. The word *cruller* comes from a Dutch word meaning "to curl," but the Dutch joked that crullers were named for Bastiaen Krol, a man who became governor of New Netherland after Peter Minuit.

The Dutch had special foods for special occasions. On Sinterklaas (Santa Claus) Day they ate *speculaas* (spicy cakes) and *borstplaat* (Sinterklaas candies). On New Year's Eve they enjoyed *sneeuwballen* (whipped cream snowballs) and *oliebollen* (fruit-filled doughnuts). The Dutch even ate special cakes right after funerals. The cakes were called *doed-koecks*, meaning "dead-cakes."

Water was not a popular drink in colonial days, mainly because it was difficult to obtain a clean, fresh supply. Beer was the most popular beverage among adults, and milk was the drink for children. Cider, made from apples, was enjoyed by everyone.

New Amsterdammers certainly did not spend all their time eating and drinking. They were a hard-working people. From sunrise to well past sunset, Dutch mothers cooked, made clothes and candles, cleaned house, and cared for the children. Many men were merchants and store owners. They operated tobacco and butcher shops, taverns, dry goods stores, and bakeries. Some earned their living by trading for furs with the Indians. They shipped the furs to Europe, where they brought large sums of money. Still other men worked as teachers, ministers, lawyers, innkeepers, blacksmiths, brewers, and millers.

Although the women generally ran the homes and the men usually ran the businesses, it did not always work that way. A number of women took over their husbands' businesses after the men died. A few New Amsterdam women operated their own tavern and hotel businesses and worked as lawyers or fur traders.

Dutch mothers and fathers were very close to their children and spent a great deal of time with them. To inform neighbors of a birth in the family, Dutch parents tied a blue ribbon to their front door if the child was a boy and a white ribbon if it was a girl. As soon as they were able, girls helped their mothers with the housework, while boys chopped wood for the fireplace, helped with the gardening, and assisted their fathers in their shops and stores.

Education was extremely important to the Dutch. In the English colonies, the educational system focused on the boys, but in New Amsterdam both sexes were fairly well educated. Children attended school three hours each morning and three hours each afternoon, every day of the year except Saturdays, Sundays, and holidays. In other words they attended school about 250 instead of the approximately 180 days that most American children now spend each year in school.

A typical New Amsterdam school was a single room with a chair and desk for the teacher and benches for the students. The older boys usually sat up front, with younger boys behind them and the girls in the back. Children learned reading from ABC *boeken* (books), arithmetic, and penmanship. A great deal of the time was also spent on religion and prayer. On Sundays the children were tested in church to ensure that the schoolmaster had taught them their religious lessons properly.

Children did not always behave like angels. At one school, the teacher complained that the students "beat each other and tore the clothes from each other's backs." Naughty schoolchildren were whipped with willow rods, forced to sit on tacks, or made to stand on tables holding heavy books above their heads. Children also played some pranks out on the streets. At night boys sometimes yelled "*Wilden!*" which means "the wild ones"—the Dutch name for the Indians. Their cries made the rattle watchmen think that Indians were attacking.

Several holidays brightened the lives of New Amsterdam children. For many, the yearly highlight was Sinterklaas Eve and Day, December 5 and 6. On Sinterklaas Eve, a jolly old bearded man in a long robe visited children's homes and asked them if they had been good that year. This old man may have looked like the children's uncle or father, but he claimed to be Sinterklaas, whom the English called St. Nicholas. After the children went to sleep, Sinterklaas returned to their homes and left them presents. The Sinterklaas tradition spread to the English colonies, but the English people said the word Sinterklaas so quickly that his name was changed to Santa Claus. The English also moved the time of Santa's visits from December 5–6 to Christmas Eve, the night of December 24–25.

Dutch skater

Another winter holiday was First Skating Day, when the ice on the ponds was safe enough to support skaters. School was closed, and children as well as adults spent the day on the ice.

Easter was a highlight of the spring. Sometime before Easter Sunday, children colored eggs using dyes made from tree bark and plants. For Easter breakfast they ate some of their colored eggs and used others in an egg-cracking game. In this game, the children tapped their eggs together and the one whose egg didn't crack could collect a whole basketful of eggs from the other players.

In the fall the Kermis festival, which resembled a modern-day county fair, was held in New Amsterdam. People from as far away as Connecticut and New Jersey brought their live-stock, prize vegetables, and manufactured goods to the large field that the English later called Bowling Green. This field still exists not far from the New York Stock Exchange. Buying, selling, and trading took place during the Kermis festival, which lasted several weeks. There were music and dancing for the adults and teenagers and puppet shows, jugglers, clowns, and toy booths for the children.

New Amsterdammers enjoyed sports and games. They brought the sport of bowling with them from The Netherlands. At first it was called ninepins or Dutch pins and was played on Bowling Green. When a law was passed banning ninepins on Sundays and holidays, the Dutch found a way around it. Since there was no law against tenpins, the Dutch added another pin.

Bowling was a favorite pastime.

Because of that, bowling is generally played with ten pins today.

Horse racing was another popular sport among New Amsterdammers. The races were held beyond the town on level areas that were made into tracks. Boat racing, skating, sleighing, tennis, backgammon, cardplaying, chess, and billiards were other popular games and sports.

Even after Peter Stuyvesant cracked down on the people's habits, New Amsterdam still had

A tavern, 1650

many problems. Ministers complained that some people were living with members of the opposite sex without being married. The town had a number of prostitutes, pirates, drunks, gamblers, and street fighters. But the ugliest aspect of the town was slavery. The Dutch West India Company owned a large number of black slaves who did manual labor and farm work in New Amsterdam. Some private citizens also had slaves. Governor Stuyvesant himself had about fifty slaves.

New Amsterdammers were very interested in politics and were continually trying to obtain more of a voice in their government. Until 1653 the town of New Amsterdam and the colony of New Netherland shared the same government. Basically, the governor's word was law. The people of New Amsterdam gained some self-rule in 1653, when they were allowed to have a *schout* (sheriff). They were also allowed five *schepens* (aldermen) and two *burgomasters* (mayors) in the town government. Governor Stuyvesant insisted on appointing the first group of officials himself, but the people protested and were soon given the right to help select these officials. In 1664, when English warships arrived and demanded that New Netherland be surrendered to England, these officials helped avoid bloodshed.

LIFE IN THE COUNTRYSIDE

In 1660 New Amsterdam was home to about a thousand people. The other four thousand who lived in what is now New York State lived in about thirty towns and villages located mainly near the Hudson River and on Long Island. Even as late as the 1770s, very few colonists lived in what is today the western half of New York State.

Fort Orange, located about 150 miles north of New Amsterdam on the Hudson River, had about

An early settlement
in Albany

one hundred people as early as the 1640s. They lived in several dozen wooden houses and farms built near the fort along the river. In 1652 Stuyvesant laid out a village named Beverwyck (Town of the Beaver, in Dutch) for these colonists. Beverwyck grew into the city of Albany, which is now the capital of New York State.

Another of the Hudson River towns was settled in the 1640s by a wealthy young Dutchman named Adriaen Van der Donck, who was the colony's first lawyer and historian. Van der Donck built a sawmill on the Hudson just a few miles north of present-day New York City. Since Van der Donck was nicknamed the "Jonkheer," meaning "Young Lord," the settlement that grew around his sawmill was called the Jonkheer's town. Just as they changed Sinterklaas to Santa Claus, the English colonists changed *Jonkheer's* to *Yonkers*. Other towns near the Hudson River included Esopus, which is today Kingston, and Schenectady.

Long Island was dotted with towns by the mid-1600s. The Dutch for the most part lived on the western end of the island. The *Janikens* (Johnnies), as the Dutch called the English, dominated eastern Long Island.

Esopus was an important settlement between Fort Orange and New Amsterdam.

Life was much slower and quieter in villages than it was in towns.

Life in the small towns and villages was much different than it was in New Amsterdam. The villagers lived more like pioneers than like city people. Instead of hiring workmen to build their homes, they cut down trees and built wooden farmhouses themselves. Often they held house-raisings in which families who already lived in an area helped newcomers build their farmhouses. The frontier people found it more difficult to obtain goods from The Netherlands or from England, so they often made their own clothes, furniture, and other household items. In many cases, they even educated their children themselves.

Life on the frontier was much more dangerous than it was in New Amsterdam, where the colonists had the protection of a fort and soldiers. If the Indians decided to strike, there was little the frontier people could do about it. In 1663, for example, the Indians massacred several dozen colonists and took nearly fifty of them captive at Esopus.

Since it was more dangerous, why did people choose to live on the frontier rather than in New Amsterdam? Some of the frontier people were fur traders who remained friendly with the Indians even when the native Americans were angry at the other white settlers. Some frontiersmen were married to Indian women and liked living close to their wives' families. There were also a few missionaries who were trying to bring Christianity to the Indians on the frontier. And of course there were a number of people who simply preferred frontier life—despite all its risks—to living in noisy, crowded New Amsterdam.

Colonists traded with Indians.

Governor Stuyvesant surrendered New Amsterdam to the English after seeing the massive fleet of warships anchored in the bay.

Chapter VI

The English Take Over

*His majesty of Great Britain, whose Right and Title
to these Parts of America is unquestionable . . .
requires a Surrender of all such Forts, Towns or
places of Strength, which are now possessed by the
Dutch.*

*English message demanding the surrender
of New Netherland in summer of 1664*

Governor Peter Stuyvesant constantly pestered
the Dutch West India Company to send more
soldiers and money to New Netherland. "Other-
wise," he wrote in 1663, "it is wholly out of our
power to keep the sinking ship afloat any longer."
The colony was in danger of sinking for several
reasons, one of which was the periodic trouble
with the Indians. The country of England posed
an even greater threat.

The English wanted to add New Netherland to
their string of colonies along America's east coast.
English lawmakers insisted that John Cabot had
claimed North America for England back in 1497
and that even Henry Hudson had been English. In
1652 The Netherlands and England went to war

over control of various lands and seas. From time to time rumors spread through New Netherland that the English were coming to seize the colony. But the Dutch West India Company could not afford to send the soldiers that Stuyvesant wanted for defense. It was said the government of The Netherlands simply did not care enough about the colony to send help. New Netherland was just one of many Dutch colonies around the world—and not a very important one at that.

In 1660 Charles II became king of England. Four years later, Charles gave his brother, James, the land the Dutch called New Netherland. Charles told his brother to take the land by force if the Dutch would not surrender it peacefully.

James, who was known as the Duke of York and Albany, organized a fleet of warships under the command of Colonel Richard Nicolls. Carrying three hundred soldiers, the ships left England in May of 1664. They anchored near New Amsterdam in August of that year and aimed their big guns at the town.

Colonel Nicolls sent a letter to Governor Stuyvesant demanding that he surrender New Netherland. The sheriff, mayors, aldermen, and almost everyone else in New Amsterdam wanted Stuyvesant to surrender peacefully, because they

King Charles II

clearly had no chance against the English. All of New Netherland had only about 10,000 colonists and 350 soliders. The English had about 100,000 people and many hundreds of soldiers in their colonies. Not only that, but Fort Amsterdam was short on the gunpowder needed to fire its big guns.

Despite the fact that the English and even his own people were against him, Stuyvesant at first refused to surrender. When Stubborn Pete prepared to fire the fort's cannons at the British ships, the people presented him with a petition begging him to surrender so as not to shed innocent blood. The governor's own seventeen-year-old son was among the ninety-three people who had signed the petition.

Seeing that he stood alone, Peter Stuyvesant ordered the white flag of surrender raised over the fort, saying that "I had rather be carried to my grave!" On September 8, 1664, Peter Stuyvesant signed the documents that officially handed New Netherland over to the English.

English names were given to the former Dutch colony. Part of the territory was named New Jersey after the island of Jersey in the English Channel. Part became officially known as Delaware, after the English Lord De La Warr. Connecticut retained its Indian name but came totally under English control.

The largest part of the territory was renamed New York, after James, the Duke of York and Albany. The towns of New Amsterdam and Beverwyck each got part of the Duke's title. New Amsterdam became New York City, and Beverwyck became Albany.

The change from Dutch to English rule of New York was a major event in American history. It paved the way for England to eventually rule the entire east coast of the present-day United States, except Florida, by the early 1700s. But it was also a very peaceful takeover. The English and the Dutch had always lived together fairly peacefully in New York. They had intermarried so extensively that many people had both English and Dutch blood and spoke both languages. By the terms of the surrender, the people of New York continued living almost exactly as they had under Dutch rule.

One change was that the colony now had an English governor, Richard Nicolls. He was a fair man who became very popular with almost everyone. Under Nicolls, the English and the Dutch even shared the same church building in New York City. After the Dutch used the building

Richard Nicholls was the first English governor of New Amsterdam.

on Sunday morning, the English would use it for their services.

Nine years after the English took over, an odd thing happened in New York. In August of 1673, while The Netherlands and England were fighting another of their wars, a Dutch fleet under Admiral Cornelis Evertsen sailed into New York Harbor. Admiral Evertsen demanded that the English surrender the colony to The Netherlands. When English officials asked by what authority Evertsen was making this demand, the Dutch admiral pointed to his ships' guns and said, "By their authority!" England returned New York to the Dutch, but just temporarily. By a peace treaty made several months later, New York was returned to the English in 1674. It remained an English colony for more than a century after that.

Sir Edmund Andros

Thomas Dongan

Soon after the English retook New Netherland in 1674, Sir Edmund Andros was appointed governor of New York by James, who had been given the colony by King Charles II, his brother. During his governorship Andros cleaned up the city and built streets and markets. He was very unpopular, however, because he was as stern and stubborn as Stuyvesant at a time when New Yorkers were clamoring for a much larger say in their government. Due to various disputes with the colonists, Andros was recalled as governor in 1681.

In 1683 a new governor, Thomas Dongan, was sent to New York with instructions from James to set up an elected general assembly. James did not really want to grant more power to the people, but he thought that allowing them more say in the government might stop their complaining. Delegates from across the colony were elected to the New York General Assembly, which first met in New York City in fall of 1683.

The assembly was not at all what we would call a democratic institution. Only male landowners could vote for the assembly members, and most of those members were wealthy men. Although the assembly had some decision-making powers, most of the authority remained with the governor, who acted in James's interests. For example, although the assembly could pass laws, the laws had to be approved by the governor. And although the assembly had the right to tax New Yorkers, the governor still controlled how the tax money was spent.

In 1685 King Charles II died and was succeeded by his brother James, who then became King James II. Since James had allowed New Yorkers a little self-government during his days as the Duke of York and Albany, they hoped that he would grant them even more power now that he was king. The opposite happened. King James II abolished the assemblies and other self-governing bodies in Connecticut, Massachusetts, New Hampshire, New Jersey, New York, Rhode Island, and Plymouth (part of present-day Massachusetts). He united these colonies into a single province called the Dominion of New England, which had Boston, Massachusetts, as its capital.

King James II

In 1686, the year that James II formed the Dominion of New England, he appointed his old friend Sir Edmund Andros as its governor. The former New York governor soon earned a reputation as one of the most hated English officials in colonial American history. He imposed higher taxes and jailed those who protested.

Governor Andros
in Boston

Meanwhile, across the Atlantic Ocean, King James II was also very unpopular. In late 1688 he was overthrown by Mary II, his own daughter, and her husband William III. In those days it took several months for news from Europe to reach the American colonies by ship. In the spring of 1689, when they learned that King James II had been overthrown, Bostonians seized his friend Governor Andros as well as other British officials. Andros was sent home to England, and soon the colonies comprising the Dominion of New England separated and resumed their limited self-government.

Governor Andros had made Captain Francis Nicholson his lieutenant-governor in the New

York Colony. With Andros deposed, Nicholson automatically became New York governor. However, a number of New Yorkers who wanted more of a role in government rallied around Jacob Leisler, a German-born soldier who had worked for the Dutch West India Company. In 1689 Leisler led a revolt in which the middle-class people took control of New York City and deposed Francis Nicholson as governor. The people then made Leisler the new governor of New York.

Under Leisler the less-wealthy New Yorkers were better off than before. More of them were allowed to vote and serve as public officials, and taxes were imposed more fairly. Jacob Leisler also dealt very well with a major emergency.

In 1689 the first of the French and Indian Wars began. During these wars the French and their Indian allies attacked many American towns. After the French and the Indians attacked Schenectady, New York, in February of 1690, Leisler thought that the colonies had to cooperate to defend themselves. He invited a number of colonies to send representatives to a meeting in New York City to discuss his idea.

Massachusetts, Plymouth, Connecticut, and New York sent representatives to this meeting, which was held in May of 1690. It was the first time that representatives of several American colonies had gathered to discuss a common problem. Connecticut even sent troops to help defend New York.

Most of New York's wealthy landowners and merchants hated Leisler because he had diminished their power. Officials in England also opposed Leisler because he had not been appointed by them. About the time that the first intercolonial congress was being held in New York City, King William III appointed Henry Sloughter governor of New York. Major Richard Ingoldsby was sent to the colony ahead of Sloughter.

Ingoldsby arrived in New York City in January of 1691. He ordered Jacob Leisler to surrender the fort. Leisler wasn't sure what to do, because Ingoldsby did not have papers to prove his authority. Finally Leisler refused to surrender and told Ingoldsby to disperse his men before there was trouble. In the battle that followed, two of Ingoldsby's soldiers were killed and several were wounded.

Governor Sloughter arrived in New York in March and arrested Leisler, his son-in-law, and several of his followers on charges of treason. The others were eventually released, but Leisler and

Showing no mercy, Governor Sloughter signed Jacob Leisler's death warrant.

his son-in-law, Jacob Milborne, were given a gruesome sentence by Governor Sloughter:

> [They shall be hanged] by the Neck and being Alive their bodys be Cutt downe to the Earth and Their Bowells be taken out and they being Alive, burnt before their faces; [then] their heads shall be struck off and their Bodys Cutt in four parts.

On May 16, 1691, Leisler and his son-in-law were led to the gallows. In his last moments, Leisler said:

> So far from revenge do we depart this world that we . . . make it our dying request to all our relations and friends, that they should in time to come be forgetful of any injury done to us.

Then the sentence was carried out, putting a tragic finish to Leisler's Rebellion.

A painting of the quaint town of New Amsterdam

Chapter VII

Indian Wars, Pirates, and Newspapers

No nation ever lost the liberty of freely speaking, writing, or publishing, but immediately lost all their liberties and became slaves. Anyone who is against freedom of the press is an enemy to his country.

John Peter Zenger, New York Weekly Journal, November 19, 1733

Under English rule New York's population continued to increase slowly. By 1690 the New York colony had 14,000 non-Indian people. In contrast, Massachusetts had over 55,000 and Virginia about 53,000 colonists. One reason New York grew so slowly was that much of its best land was owned by wealthy people. Europeans who settled in America usually chose places where they could obtain good land more easily. In addition the New York frontier was very vulnerable to Indian attack.

By the late 1680s, France, England's long-time enemy, was preparing to join with the Indians in attacks on the American colonies. England and France both controlled lands in North America.

France ruled part of Canada, which it called New France. England ruled its colonies along the east coast of what is now the United States. Each country wanted to take over the other's North American lands. Both were interested in a vast amount of land in what is today the middle of the United States.

Ever since Samuel de Champlain had led them in an attack on the Iroquois in 1609, the Algonquians had been friendly with the French. Algonquian Indians met with the French in Canada and agreed to help the French when they attacked the English colonies. In 1689–90 French and Indian raiders swept down from Canada and attacked New York, New Hampshire, and Massachusetts. These three areas were targeted because of their relative closeness to French headquarters in Canada.

One of the worst of these attacks occurred on the night of February 8, 1690, in Schenectady, New York. Schenectady was protected by a tall wooden fence, but it was reported that on the night of the attack the only "guards" at the gate were two snowmen. The French and the Indians entered the town, murdered more than sixty people, took about thirty prisoners, and burned nearly every house to the ground.

People fleeing the attack on Schenectady, February 8, 1690. Some colonists, wearing only their night clothes, trudged through cold and snow to reach safety in Albany.

The attacks on New York, New Hampshire, and Massachusetts began what are called the French and Indian Wars. The names and dates of these wars were:

King William's War (1689–1697)

Queen Anne's War (1702–1713)

King George's War (1744–1748)

The French and Indian War (1754–1763)

Ever since they had been shot at by Samuel de Champlain, the Iroquois Indians had hated the French. Because of this, some of the Iroquois fought alongside the English and the American colonists as they battled the French and their Algonquian allies.

The struggle between France and England was not settled until the final conflict, the French and

William Johnson

Robert Rogers

Indian War. By the time this war broke out, the English had built a number of forts in New York. Much of the fighting occurred at or near the New York forts. These forts were intended to block the French and the Indians from entering strategic colonial regions.

A New York man named William Johnson played an important role in helping the English win the French and Indian War. Johnson was friendly with the Iroquois Indians, and he convinced some of them to fight on the English side. In September of 1755, Major General Johnson led an army consisting of three thousand militiamen (emergency armed forces) and three hundred Mohawk and Oneida Indians against a large French force at Lake George in New York. In one of the bloodiest battles of the French and Indian War, the English forces defeated the French forces at the Battle of Lake George.

Robert Rogers of New Hampshire also participated in a number of key battles in New York during the French and Indian War. Rogers commanded a group of fighting men known as Rogers' Rangers. The Rangers fought Indian-style, making sneak attacks and hiding behind trees instead of fighting out in the open as European armies did. Rogers' Rangers helped the English eventually capture forts Niagara, Ticonderoga, and Crown Point in New York in the summer of 1759. These victories helped the British ultimately defeat the French. The peace treaty made between the British and the French in 1763 transferred Canada and all French possessions east of the Mississippi River (except New Orleans, Louisiana), to the British.

Even before the first of the French and Indian Wars, the British began passing a series of laws called Navigation Acts. These helped turn New York into a haven for smugglers and pirates. The Navigation Acts were a series of tax laws and other measures that made it difficult for the colonists to trade legally with any non-English country. The British wanted the colonists to buy goods only from them. However, just as people today shop at stores that offer the best buys, the colonists bought goods from countries that gave them the best deals. This meant that sometimes they purchased English goods but that other times they bought goods from The Netherlands and other countries.

Many colonists ignored the Navigation Acts and smuggled goods from non-English countries into Boston, Massachusetts, and into New York City. The ships carrying the smuggled goods were unloaded in the middle of the night, or at remote places far from the sight of English officials. Since the colonists felt that the British Navigation Acts had forced people to turn to smuggling, few of them considered it wrong to buy or sell smuggled goods.

Piracy was another way that New Yorkers obtained goods cheaply. Pirates robbed ships belonging to nations that were enemies of England. They brought the goods to New York City where they were sold to wealthy merchants. The merchants in turn sold the goods at relatively low prices to the townspeople. However, many pirates did not just rob ships belonging to enemy nations. They also robbed vessels belonging to neutral nations and even ships belonging to English merchants.

Except for the shipowners, just about everyone gained. The pirate captains made a fortune. The merchants who bought the stolen goods got richer. The townspeople were able to buy goods for less than the usual price. It was common knowledge that Benjamin Fletcher, governor of the New York Colony from 1692 to 1697, accepted bribes and presents from the pirate captains. And since the pirates spent their gold and silver freely, they were also well-liked by New York City's tavern

British Captain Edward Teach, better known as the fierce pirate, "Blackbeard" owners and shopkeepers. During the late 1600s pirates were a common sight on New York City's streets.*

In 1695 the English government asked a New York shipowner and sea captain named William Kidd to fight the pirates. But instead of capturing the buccaneers, Kidd was accused of becoming a pirate himself. By the mid-1690s pirates even robbed ships on the Hudson River between New York City and Albany. Pirates continued to frequent New York City until the early 1700s.

By 1720 the New York Colony was home to about 37,000 people, about 7,000 of whom lived in and very near to New York City. The people of the colony were eager to find out what was happening in England and in other parts of America. In 1725 a printer named William Bradford began publishing the colony's first newspaper, the *New-York Gazette*, in New York City. Bradford was the official printer for the New York government, and so the *Gazette* reflected the views of Governor William Cosby and of the colony's wealthy merchants.

William Bradford

Bradford was assisted by a German-born printer named John Peter Zenger, who felt that the *Gazette* was not reporting the truth. Zenger thought that Cosby was just another in a series of

* A map of Manhattan in 1695 appears on page 148

greedy and corrupt New York governors who squandered and stole public funds and deprived most of the people of their rights. With the help of some of Governor Cosby's enemies, Zenger established a rival newspaper, the *New York Weekly Journal*, in 1733.

The *Journal* printed poems and articles that were very critical of Governor Cosby and other corrupt New York officials. It printed what appeared to be advertisements about lost animals that were really descriptions of New York officials. For example, the sheriff was characterized as "a monkey of the larger sort, about four feet high." Another official was described as "a large spaniel, of about five feet five inches high." And the governor himself was called a "rogue" who needed to be placed on a leash. The *Journal* became very popular with many of the less-wealthy people of New York City, who agreed with Zenger.

Governor Cosby, however, was outraged. As a warning to Zenger, the governor had several copies of the *Journal* publicly burned. When that did not scare Zenger, the governor had him arrested in November of 1734 and charged him with treason.* While in jail Zenger gave instructions to his wife through a hole in the prison door, and she continued to publish his newspaper.

* A copy of the proclamation issued against Zenger appears on page 149

Treason was an extremely serious charge, as Jacob Leisler had learned forty-three years earlier. Although Zenger was to have a jury trial, several aspects of the case seemed to be what we would call "fixed." The judge, New York Chief Justice James De Lancey, was a good friend of Governor Cosby. When Zenger's lawyers argued that the judge was prejudiced against their client, De Lancey took away their licenses to practice law. He then appointed a rather weak lawyer to represent Zenger.

The burning of Zenger's weekly journal at Wall Street, November 6, 1734

The Zenger trial opened at City Hall on August 4, 1735. The government lawyer explained that ridiculing the governor was treason and that Zenger should be hanged. Probably most of the people sitting in the packed courtroom, standing on the streets outside City Hall, and drinking toasts to Zenger in nearby taverns assumed that the court's verdict would find the printer guilty.

But John Peter Zenger's friends arranged for Andrew Hamilton, a well-known Philadelphia lawyer, to represent him. The elderly Hamilton gave a speech in which he defended Zenger's right to print what he considered to be the truth. Hamilton closed his defense by saying:

The question before the court—and you, gentlemen of the jury—is not of small or private concern. It is not the cause of a poor printer, nor of New York alone, which you are now trying. No! It may in its consequences affect every freeman that lives under British government on the main of America! It is the best cause. It is the cause of liberty! And I make no doubt but your upright conduct this day will not only entitle you to the love and esteem of your fellow citizens, but every man who prefers freedom to a life of slavery will bless and honor you, as men who have baffled the attempt of tyranny, and by an impartial and uncorrupt verdict have laid a noble foundation for securing to ourselves, our posterity, and our neighbors, that to which nature and the laws of our country have given us a right—the liberty both of exposing and opposing power—in these parts of the world, at least—by speaking and writing truth!

When Hamilton finished speaking, people in the courtroom rose to their feet and cheered wildly. Hamilton's repeated references to "liberty" and "freedom," as opposed to "slavery" and "tyranny," would be heard years later by American patriots rebelling against British rule.

The jury retired and within minutes returned with the verdict: "Not guilty!" That decision made in a crowded New York courtroom in summer of 1735 was an historic triumph for those who believed in freedom of the press. After Zenger was released, he continued to publish the *New York Weekly Journal* until his death in 1746.* The newspaper was then continued by his wife and son until 1751.

* A copy of John Peter Zenger *New-York Weekly Journal* appears on page 150

Andrew Hamilton, defending freedom of the press during the John Peter Zenger trial

CAPTAIN WILLIAM KIDD (1645?–1701)

Born in Scotland, William Kidd was believed to be the son of a minister. In about 1689 Kidd settled in New York City, where he soon became a wealthy sea captain and shipowner. At the beginning of the first of the French and Indian Wars, Kidd led one of his own ships in several successful sea battles against the French.

In 1695, Kidd was visiting London when he met some prominent Englishmen including future New York governor Richard Coote, the Earl of Bellomont. The men asked Kidd to lead an expedition against the pirates who were robbing British ships near the African coast. In addition to fighting pirates, Kidd was asked to capture French ships, because England and France were still fighting in King William's War.

Captain Kidd agreed, and soon Bellomont and a number of wealthy Englishmen and New Yorkers supplied him with a new thirty-gun ship, the *Adventure Galley*. Kidd rounded up a good crew, but just as the *Adventure Galley* was leaving England, a British warship stopped it, and an officer demanded that Kidd turn over some of his men to him. The British navy had the right to do this, so Kidd reluctantly turned over some of his sailors, then headed to New York.

En route to America, Kidd had his first success when he seized a small French vessel, which he brought back with him to New York. In New York Kidd recruited more sailors, but they weren't as trustworthy as those he had lost to the English navy. Captain Kidd said good-bye to his wife and baby daughter, boarded the *Adventure Galley*, and ordered his men to sail east, toward Africa.

Captain Kidd seized two ships that were sailing under the French flag and had many other adventures during the next several years. But almost from the start, his men gave him trouble. Instead of regular pay, the men received a percentage of whatever treasure they seized. "Why limit ourselves to French ships and pirates?" the men soon said. They wanted Kidd to attack other ships—even English ones.

Kidd did his best to keep the men from taking over his ship. When a man named William Moore tried to convince the crew to mutiny, Kidd hit him on the head with a bucket, killing him. Nevertheless, Captain Kidd apparently attacked several ships he wasn't authorized to attack, and some of his men left the *Adventure Galley* and joined up with pirates.

Word reached England and America that Captain Kidd had turned pirate, and King William III and the new governor of New York, the Earl of Bellomont, put out an order for his arrest. Captain Kidd certainly did not act like a pirate when he heard that he was wanted. Expecting that Governor Bellomont and other British officials would sympathize with his problems with his crew, Kidd bought a smaller ship on a Caribbean

The elaborate home of Captain William Kidd on Tienhoven Street

island, loaded his treasure onto it, and then sailed up America's east coast. But before landing at Boston to meet with Governor Bellomont, Kidd stopped at Gardiner's Island off the New York coast, where he buried a portion of his treasure.

Captain Kidd did not receive the sympathetic treatment he had expected. Instead, he was taken to England, where he was tried for piracy and for killing mutineer William Moore. Although several outstanding lawyers prosecuted him, Kidd was not allowed to have a lawyer of his own. The defendant tried to explain that some of the charges against him were lies and that he had been forced into piracy. But he was found guilty and sentenced to be hanged. After hearing the sentence, Kidd said: "My Lord, it is a very hard sentence. For my part I am the innocentest person of them all."

The story of Captain William Kidd did not end when he was hanged on May 23, 1701. The treasure he had buried on Gardiner's Island was found, but there were rumors that he had also buried some treasure on a Caribbean island or somewhere along the shore of New York, Rhode Island, Connecticut, or Delaware. No one has ever found Captain Kidd's hidden treasure, but even today people still look for it.

The Sons of Liberty seizing British arms enroute to the city

Chapter VIII

The Revolutionary War

That Americans are entitled to freedom is incontestable. . . . No reason can be assigned why one man should exercise any power . . . over his fellow [human beings] . . . unless they have voluntarily vested him with it. Since . . . Americans have not, by any act of theirs, empowered the British Parliament to make laws for them, it follows they [the British] can have no just authority [over the Americans].

> *Alexander Hamilton, writing in late 1774*

Things will come right, and these States will be great and flourishing.

> *John Jay, writing to George Washington in spring of 1779*

During the nearly two centuries of British rule, the colonists' attitude toward England gradually changed. The early colonists had regarded themselves as English people who happened to live across the ocean from their mother country. For the most part they had been content to be ruled by lawmakers and governors sent from England. The children and grandchildren of these early colonists wanted more of a say in their government, and so England had allowed them to elect assemblies with limited powers. By the 1760s, this was not enough for many colonists. A few were even in favor of the colonies separating from England and becoming a new country.

There were several reasons for these growing feelings. By the mid-1700s the colonies were home to many thousands of less-wealthy English people and to thousands more who had come from such countries as Ireland, Scotland, Germany, The Netherlands, France, and Sweden. Most of these people had never been to Great Britain, did little or no business with the British, and felt little loyalty to England. Some were angry at Britain for not providing enough help or protection during the French and Indian Wars.

At the same time that they were turning away from Britain, the people in the various colonies were drawing closer to each other. In 1690 Jacob Leisler had organized the first intercolonial congress. In the summer of 1754, an even bigger congress was held at Albany, New York, to discuss strategy for fighting the French and Indian War. Called the Albany Congress, this meeting was attended by representatives from New York, New Hampshire, Massachusetts, Rhode Island, Connecticut, Maryland, and Pennsylvania. At this

The signatures of the twenty-five members of the Albany Congress and other meetings, the colonists found that they shared common problems, had the same interests, and even spoke and dressed similarly. They were starting to think of themselves as being one people—Americans.

Breaking away from England was a giant step, however. By the end of the French and Indian War in 1763, many Americans sought more freedom for the colonies. But few yet favored separation from Britain. Then the British lawmakers did something that started more people thinking about independence. Britain needed money to pay its war debts and to maintain an army and navy in its recently won American lands. England's law-making body, Parliament, decided that the American colonies would help pay the bills by paying extra taxes.

In 1764 Parliament passed the Sugar Act, which placed a tax on non-British molasses imported into the colonies. Then in 1765 it passed the Stamp Act, which required the colonists to buy special stamps to place on all newspapers, wills, deeds, and other legal documents.

The colonists were infuriated by these new taxes. Across the colonies, protest meetings were held in "liberty halls" and under "liberty trees." Newspapers also joined the chorus of protest. On

A sign from one of the inns where the Sons of Liberty often met

June 6, 1765, the *New-York Gazette* editorialized, "If the Welfare of the Mother country necessarily requires a Sacrifice of the most natural rights of the Colonies . . . then the connection between them ought to cease."

Colonial leaders realized that by joining together they could make a more powerful protest than if each of the thirteen colonies complained separately. In the fall of 1765, colonial leaders organized the Stamp Act Congress. Representatives from nine colonies attended this meeting, which was held in New York City in October. The Stamp Act Congress denounced the hated Stamp Act and informed British lawmakers that Americans "could not be taxed without their consent."

People did not just talk and write protests. Many struck back at Britain in a way that would hurt the most—financially. Instead of buying British tea, Americans made their own out of sassafras or mint. The *New-York Gazette* advised readers: "It is better to wear a homespun coat than to lose our liberty." The colonists agreed. They began making their own jackets, trousers, and dresses.

Throughout the colonies, shopkeepers and laborers formed patriotic clubs called the Sons of

The true Sons of Liberty

And Supporters of the Non-Importation Agreement,

ARE determined to refent any the leaft Infult or Menace offer'd to any one or more of the feveral Committees appointed by the Body at Faneuil-Hall, and chaftife any one or more of them as they deferve ; and will alfo fupport the Printers in any Thing the Committees fhall defire them to print.

☞AS a Warning to any one that fhall affront as aforefaid, upon fure Information given, one of thefe Advertifements will be pofted up at the Door or Dwelling-Houfe of the Offender.

HANDBILL OF THE TRUE SONS OF LIBERTY

Sons of Liberty posted handbills such as the one above to support their cause.

STAMP
ACT

THE FOLLY OF ENGLAND
THE RUIN OF AMERICA

Daily, colonists
demonstrated
against the Stamp
Act.

Liberty. The Sons became the muscle behind the
American protest movement. Not only did they
threaten the men who tried to distribute the
stamps, they also threatened Americans who
continued doing business with the British. The
New York City Sons of Liberty were led by
Alexander McDougall, Isaac Sears, and John
Lamb. They held demonstrations every day on
Bowling Green and on street corners. They
ransacked the home of a British officer and
attempted to capture the British fort. The patriots

even burned a dummy made to look like British acting governor Cadwallader Colden, to demonstrate their dislike of British rule.

The British had not expected the Americans to react so violently, and Parliament repealed the Stamp Act in March of 1766.

The British still wanted tax money from the Americans. They also wanted to prove that they were still in charge of the colonists. During the 1760s and 1770s, the British passed other tax laws that the Americans defied. Recalling their protests of the Navigation Acts of the 1600s, the colonists smuggled goods from non-British countries into Boston, New York City, and other ports.

Even before the Revolutionary War began, the patriots and the British soldiers, who were called redcoats, clashed. The Sons of Liberty planted a pine tree, which they called their liberty pole, in a field in New York City. They met regularly at the pole to listen to speeches about British injustice and to yell out threats to passing British soldiers. The patriots felt about their liberty pole much the same as Americans now feel about their country's flag.

Several times the British soldiers destroyed the New Yorkers' liberty pole, causing heated

Some patriots were willing to give their lives defending the liberty pole.

arguments and even fights between the two groups. On January 18, 1770, shortly after another attack on their liberty pole, the Sons of Liberty clashed with about sixty redcoats at Golden Hill, which is now John Street in New York City. A number of patriots were stabbed with bayonets and some soldiers were beaten. The fight became known as the Battle of Golden Hill, and it was one of the first violent clashes between the colonists and the British in the years before the Revolutionary War.

Much more violent anti-British demonstrations were taking place in Boston, Massachusetts, which was the hotbed of American discontent. On March 5, 1770, Bostonians threw stones at some British soldiers. The frightened soldiers fired into the crowd, killing five people. This street brawl became known as the Boston Massacre.

Nearly four years later, on December 16, 1773, about fifty Bostonians dumped 340 chests of tea into Boston Harbor to protest the tax on tea. Paul Revere, a silversmith who served as messenger for the Boston patriots, rode to New York City to report the news of this Boston Tea Party. On the night of April 22, 1774, New York City patriots held their own "tea party" by dumping eighteen boxes of British tea into the water. Other colonies also hosted "tea parties."

In towns throughout the colonies, militiamen began drilling in case they had to go to war with Great Britain. These militiamen came to be called minutemen because they could prepare for battle in sixty seconds. On the night of April 18, 1775, British troops marched from Boston to Lexington, Massachusetts. Their mission was to capture the

American leaders Sam Adams and John Hancock in Lexington, and then seize military supplies in the nearby town of Concord.

The Americans learned of the British plans, and a group of minutemen gathered on the Lexington village green. The British arrived at dawn and ordered the colonists to go home. The outnumbered minutemen started to disperse, but suddenly, a shot rang out and the redcoats began firing. In the first battle of the Revolutionary War, the Battle of Lexington, eight colonists were killed and ten were wounded. The Americans wounded one British soldier during the shooting.

As news spread of the battle at Lexington, American patriots across the Massachusetts countryside headed toward nearby Concord, where the British were assembling. This time the Americans had more soldiers than the British. In the Battle of Concord and the British retreat that followed, the patriots killed or wounded nearly three hundred redcoats while losing about one hundred of their own men. Fought several hours after the Battle of Lexington on the morning of April 19, 1775, the Battle of Concord was the first American victory of the Revolution.

After these opening battles, the colonists divided into three groups. Probably a little more than one-third of the colonists were Whigs—people who wanted America to free itself from Great Britain. Probably less than a third were Loyalists or Tories—people who sided with Britain. The final third were neutral and hoped that the two other groups would settle their differences.

Most of the wealthier colonists were Loyalists because they did a great deal of business with Britain and had other ties with the mother country. Because it was home to so many merchants and wealthy landowners, New York had the most Loyalists of any of the thirteen colonies. About 40,000 Loyalists left New York during the Revolutionary War era.

Shortly after Paul Revere brought them news of the battles of Lexington and Concord, American patriots seized control of New York City. They helped themselves to firearms and other supplies from British warehouses, and they took charge of the governments of New York City and of the entire colony. Eventually, they forced British governor William Tryon to flee to a British warship in New York Harbor.

Less than a month after the war broke out, a Vermont man named Ethan Allen and a Connecticut man named Benedict Arnold led about eighty

Ethan Allen captures Fort Ticonderoga.

Vermont soldiers known as Green Mountain Boys in an attack on Fort Ticonderoga in northeastern New York. At dawn of May 10, 1775, the Green Mountain Boys charged the fort, awoke the British soldiers, and demanded that they surrender. When the British commander asked who was ordering the surrender, Ethan Allen was reported to have answered, "In the name of the great Jehovah and the Continental Congress!" By Jehovah he meant God. The Continental Congress was a temporary government the colonists had set up during the Revolutionary War era.

Without a shot being fired, the Americans captured Fort Ticonderoga and its more than one hundred cannons. Two days later, on May 12, 1775, Seth Warner, Ethan Allen's cousin, led a group of New Englanders in the capture of the British fort at Crown Point, New York.

On June 17, 1775 the British, despite terrible losses, won the Battle of Bunker Hill, near Boston, Massachusetts. A few days later, George Washington of Virginia took command of the American army, which was called the Continental Army. John Adams of Massachusetts soon advised Washington that New York was "a kind of key to the whole continent." Adams said this because New York Harbor was one of America's most important ports and because, if the patriots could control New York's interior, the redcoats could be prevented from sweeping down through the area from Canada.

Although the British had abandoned New York City, George Washington knew they would try to retake it. In spring of 1776 General Washington arrived in New York City with thousands of American soldiers. Washington ordered his men to build forts, barricades, and trenches to protect the city from the expected British assault. In what was the biggest military expedition Britain

Charles Wilson Peale's painting of George Washington at the age of forty, wearing the uniform of a Virginian colonel

116

launched up to that time, nearly 500 British ships carrying 32,000 men began to arrive in New York Harbor in the summer of 1776.

By this time the bitter fighting between the British and the colonists had convinced most of the 2.5 million Americans that it was time to separate from the mother country. In summer of 1776 the Continental Congress in Philadelphia created a Declaration of Independence to explain why the colonies, or United States as they now called themselves, should be free of Britain's rule. The Continental Congress adopted the Declaration of Independence on July 4, 1776, the date

Signing of the Declaration of Independence, engraving by W.L. Ormsby, from a painting by John Trumbull

Patriots destroy the statue of George III, that stood in Bowling Green.

Americans celebrate as their nation's birthday. Of the fifty-six members of Congress who signed the Declaration, four were from New York. They were William Floyd, Philip Livingston, Francis Lewis, and Lewis Morris, and their signatures can be seen at the top of the declaration's fifth column.*

To inspire his troops General Washington ordered the declaration read to them on July 9, 1776—a date that is still important in New York

* A copy of the Declaration of Independence appears on page 151

history. On that day New York lawmakers met in White Plains and approved the declaration. That same night, New York patriots pulled down the statue of Britain's King George III that stood in Bowling Green. The statue was melted and made into more than 40,000 bullets, which the Americans later directed against the redcoats.

The expected British attack on New York City finally began in late August of 1776. On August 27 twenty thousand British troops fought ten thousand Americans in the Battle of Long Island, which took place in what is now Brooklyn. While watching this battle from a hilltop, George Washington sadly said: "Good God! What brave fellows I must this day lose!"

Washington's words proved true. The British killed, wounded, or took prisoner fifteen hundred Americans while losing about four hundred men

In 1776, a British officer painted this scene of Howe's fleet anchored off Long Island.

The Battle of Long Island shows the Americans retreating.

themselves during the Battle of Long Island. A fog prevented the British from capturing additional patriots. At a point where the Brooklyn Bridge now stands, the Americans boarded boats and escaped to the island of Manhattan.

After losing the Battle of Long Island, Washington tried to hold Manhattan, but many of his soldiers deserted. On September 15 the British seized much of Manhattan as Washington's troops ran away from the advancing enemy. The

British forces almost captured George Washington too. Washington was so angry at seeing his men running away that he stayed too long on the battlefield and was nearly captured by some Hessians—German soldiers hired to fight for the British.

The Continental Congress had discussed, but rejected, the idea of burning New York City to the ground to prevent the British from occupying it. However, several days after the British took Manhattan, a fire broke out and destroyed a quarter of the city. Although the cause of the fire

The fire in New York City, September 20, 1776, destroyed five hundred buildings before it finally burned out.

was never learned, George Washington commented: "Providence [God] or some good honest fellow has done more for us than we were disposed to do for ourselves." But the fire did not drive the British from the city. Instead, thousands of Loyalists from throughout the colonies flocked to the city. The British held New York City for seven years, until the very end of the war.

On September 21, 1776, the day that the fire began, a young Connecticut man named Nathan Hale was arrested by the British near New York City. The twenty-one-year-old Hale had disguised himself as a Dutch schoolmaster, but he had really been spying on the British. Nathan Hale was sentenced to be hanged the next day. "I only regret that I have but one life to lose for my country," he was reported to have calmly said, just before dying. Because of those words, Nathan Hale came to represent the ultimate patriot to many Americans.

Ninety-two of the 308 battles of the Revolutionary War were fought in New York. In fact, more Revolutionary War battles took place in New York than in any other colony. In the summer and early fall of 1777, the Americans earned three of their greatest victories—the battles of Oriskany, Bennington, and Saratoga—in New York.

Nathan Hale

British, Hessian, and Iroquois soldiers gathered at Fort Oswego, New York before their assault on Fort Stanwix.

In the war about 1,600 Iroquois Indians fought on the British side, while only about 250 fought with the Americans. In the summer of 1777, the British Colonel Barry Saint Leger led about 1,200 British, Hessian, and Iroquois soldiers out of Oswego, New York. They headed east toward Albany, where St. Leger planned to meet up with a larger force under the command of the British General John Burgoyne. The combined forces were to capture Albany and the rest of New York's Hudson River Valley, the area that John Adams thought was a "key to the whole continent."

On the way to Albany, St. Leger and his men arrived at Fort Stanwix near Oriskany, New York. Fort Stanwix was held by only five hundred Americans, but they refused to surrender. Meanwhile, American Brigadier General Nicholas Herkimer approached Fort Stanwix with eight hundred New York militiamen. Near Oriskany, Herkimer's forces and St. Leger's troops fought one of the Revolution's bloodiest battles on August 6, 1777.

For six hours the American and British forces slaughtered each other with bayonets, muskets, and tomahawks. During the fighting a musket shot shattered General Herkimer's leg below the knee. Although he later died of his wounds, General Herkimer continued to direct the American forces while leaning against the trunk of a tree. By the time the British were forced to retreat, each side had suffered about two hundred deaths. The Americans were considered the victors because St. Leger was prevented from taking Fort Stanwix. St. Leger had to return to Oswego instead of going on to help General Burgoyne in his attempt to capture the Albany region.

Ten days after the Battle of Oriskany, American forces under Major General John Stark of New

Hampshire defeated the British in another important battle, the Battle of Bennington. The battle was actually fought to the northwest of Bennington, Vermont, near what is now Walloomsac, New York. So fierce was the fighting at the Battle of Bennington that General Stark said it sounded "like one continued clap of thunder." The Americans killed or wounded two hundred British troops and captured seven hundred others, while suffering about eighty casualties themselves. The battles of Bennington and Oriskany paved the way for the Americans to win the even more crucial Battle of Saratoga, which is often called the most important battle of the Revolutionary War.

General John Stark

British General John Burgoyne was more successful in New York than were Barry St. Leger and other British leaders. In July of 1777 Burgoyne's forces retook Fort Ticonderoga, which Ethan Allen and Benedict Arnold had captured two years earlier. Burgoyne and his men also captured other New York forts and settlements. In mid-September, Burgoyne led his 8,500-man army to the Saratoga Lake area in eastern New York, about thirty miles north of Albany. He still hoped to capture the area, along with the rest of the Hudson River Valley.

Meanwhile, the Americans were gathering more men to defend New York. Six thousand Americans, under the command of General Horatio Gates, waited for Burgoyne's troops near the town of Saratoga, which is now Schuylerville. On September 19, 1777, at a place called Freeman's Farm, the American and the British forces fought a fierce battle that temporarily halted the British in their march toward Albany. The redcoats lost about six hundred and the Americans about three hundred men.

Eighteen days later, on October 7, 1777, the British made a second attack on the American soldiers at Freeman's Farm. The result was similar to the first battle. This time the British lost 600, while the Americans lost only 150 men.

Burgoyne and his men could not escape, because the growing American army surrounded them after the second Freeman's Farm fight. On October 17, 1777, General Burgoyne and his five-thousand-man army surrendered to General Horatio Gates at Saratoga. The two battles fought at Freeman's Farm are generally called the First and Second Battles of Freeman's Farm. But the entire engagement, including Burgoyne's surrender, is usually called the Battle of Saratoga.

The Battle of Saratoga

The American victory at Saratoga is considered the war's turning point. It prevented the British from taking control of the Hudson River Valley. It left five thousand British soldiers unable to fight for the rest of the war. It also persuaded France, Britain's old enemy, that the Americans had a chance to win their revolution. In the spring of 1778, France entered the war on the American side. Their soldiers, sailors, ships, weapons, and money helped the Americans to win the Revolutionary War.

John Trumbull's sketch captures the agony in the faces of starving Americans who were imprisoned in the British ship *Jersey* anchored off Brooklyn.

Before that final victory, the Americans had many difficult times. About ten thousand Americans—about as many as died in combat—died in the English prison ships anchored off the shore of New York City. Jammed together in these ships, the Americans succumbed to hunger, thirst, and a variety of diseases.

On New York's frontier, meanwhile, pro-British Iroquois under the famous warrior Joseph Brant and the American settlers were raiding each other's villages and killing each other in large numbers. The Iroquois threat was ended in 1779, when General John Sullivan and General James Clinton commanded troops that slaughtered the People of the Longhouse and destroyed their villages over a wide area of central and western New York. The raids by Sullivan and Clinton ended the days when the Iroquois were a major force in New York.

The final battle of the Revolutionary War took place at Yorktown, Virginia, where George Washington's seventeen-thousand-man army forced British General Charles Cornwallis and his eight-thousand men to surrender on October 19, 1781.

At Yorktown, French and American forces fought the British for almost a month before the British surrendered.

A drawing of the last boatload of British soldiers leaving New York in 1783

After this great victory, the Americans were assured victory in the Revolution. Finally, on November 25, 1783, George Washington and his troops reclaimed New York City from the British. A woman who witnessed this historic event, known as Evacuation Day, later described it:

> The troops just leaving us [the British] were as if equipped for show, and with their scarlet uniforms [they] made a brilliant display. The troops that marched in [the Americans], on the contrary, were ill-clad and weather-beaten, and made a forlorn appearance. But then they were our troops, and as I looked at them, and thought upon all they had done and suffered for us, my heart and my eyes were full, and I admired and gloried in them the more because they were weather-beaten and forlorn.

Evacuation Day was an emotional day for New Yorkers and other Americans. The British were gone and the new country, the United States of America, was now truly independent.

JOSEPH BRANT (1742–1807)

Portrait of Joseph Brant by William Berczy, Jr.

Joseph Brant was one of the most important Indians in North American history. A Mohawk Indian, he was born in 1742. The boy was named *Thayendanegea*, meaning "Two Sticks of Wood Bound Together." Thayendanegea grew up in an Indian village at Canajoharie, New York, northwest of Albany. When Thayendanegea was very young, his father died and his mother married an Indian whose English name was Nicklaus Brant. To the English, Thayendanegea became known as Joseph Brant.

The people of Brant's village had a great deal of contact both with the British and the Americans. The wealthy trader William Johnson lived nearby. British missionaries regularly came to the village. Brant spent much of his boyhood hunting, spearing salmon, and swimming in the creek with several non-Indian boys who lived on a nearby farm.

In about 1753 Brant's sister, Molly, married trader William Johnson and left to live in his huge house. Even though he was just in his mid-teens at the time, Brant fought on the British side under Johnson during the French and Indian War. Joseph Brant later said he was so nervous when his first battle began that he had to hold onto a tree to keep from fainting.

In 1761 Eleazar Wheelock, who had founded a school for Indians in Lebanon, Connecticut, asked Johnson to recommend several potential students. Johnson recommended Brant for Wheelock's school, which eventually moved to New Hampshire and became Dartmouth College. During the next two years, Brant learned to pray, talk, dress, eat, and act like an English gentleman. In 1763 Joseph Brant left school and began working as an interpreter for the British and as a Christian missionary among his own people. He even translated parts of the Bible and a prayer book into the Mohawk language.

When the Revolutionary War began, Brant and most other Mohawks took the British side. They had fought for the British during the French and Indian War, and most of them loathed the Americans for taking more and more Indian lands. Brant, the seemingly peaceful man who had quaked with fear during his first battle, led Mohawks and other Iroquois on many raids in which hundreds of New York colonists were killed. He also led an Indian force that fought in the Battle of Oriskany in August of 1777.

In 1779 the American forces devastated Iroquois villages in central and western New York, and Brant and thousands of his people were homeless. The British granted Brant and his followers land along the Grand River in Ontario, Canada. Joseph Brant helped found Brant's Town there—a settlement with a church, houses, farms, and schools. The city of Brantford and the county of Brant in Ontario, Canada were named in Brant's honor.

MARGARET CORBIN (1751–1800)

Margaret Cochran, a courageous fighter in the Revolutionary War, was born on the Pennsylvania frontier, about 150 miles west of Philadelphia. She was three years old when the French and Indian War began. Two years later her father was killed and her mother taken captive in an Indian raid. Margaret went to live with an uncle.

In 1772 twenty-one-year-old Margaret married John Corbin. When the Revolutionary War broke out, Corbin joined the Pennsylvania Artillery and Margaret followed him from battle to battle.

After the Americans lost the battles of Long Island and Manhattan in the late summer of 1776, they tried to make a stand at Fort Washington. Located in northwestern Manhattan where one end of the George Washington Bridge now stands, Fort Washington was the last piece of Manhattan real estate under American control.

On November 16, 1776, the three thousand Americans in the fort were attacked by eight thousand British and Hessian soldiers. During this fierce battle, Margaret helped her husband load his cannon. Suddenly, during a charge by the Hessian soldiers, John Corbin was killed. Margaret immediately took his place and fired his cannon at the enemy. She continued to fire during this losing battle until an enemy shot smashed into her, ripping away part of her chest and nearly tearing off one of her arms.

Other women took part in the Revolutionary War as nurses, spies, and even soldiers, but Margaret Corbin was one of the first to actually fight in a battle. Little is known about the rest of Margaret Corbin's life. It is known that she suffered almost constant pain from her terrible wounds and that she lived her last years near what is now the United States Military Academy at West Point, New York.

Washington waved good-bye to his soldiers as he left New York on
December 4, 1783.

Chapter IX

The Eleventh State

. . . the situation of the General Government (if it can be called a government.) is shaken to the foundation, and liable to be overset by every blast. In a word, it is at an end, and unless a remedy is soon applied, anarchy and confusion will inevitably ensue.

George Washington, writing to Thomas Jefferson in May of 1787 about the need for a stronger federal government

For several years after the Revolution it appeared that the new country would fall apart. The United States was governed by the Articles of Confederation, an agreement that was approved by the thirteen former colonies in 1781. The Articles granted little power to the central government, and so the thirteen former colonies often acted like thirteen separate countries rather than like members of one nation.

The small United States Army, consisting of about seven hundred men, was too weak to deal with trouble. When Shays' Rebellion took place in western Massachusetts in 1786-87, the Massachusetts militia had to handle the problem because the U.S. Army couldn't deal with it. In addition, the federal government had no courts, no President to lead the country, and no power to levy taxes. Congress even lacked a permanent home, and moved about between such cities as Philadelphia in Pennsylvania, Princeton and Trenton in New Jersey, and Annapolis in Maryland. In 1785 New York City became the capital, but nobody expected that it would remain so for long.

To make things worse, the former colonies often quarreled with each other. For example, New York argued with Connecticut and New Jersey over financial matters.

It seemed likely that the United States would not stay united unless it created a stronger central government. To do so, a Constitutional Convention met in Philadelphia in 1787. Every state but Rhode Island sent delegates to this convention. New York was represented by young lawyer Alexander Hamilton, New York Supreme Court Justice Robert Yates, and Albany Mayor John Lansing.

Hamilton, Yates, and Lansing helped create the United States Constitution, a document which greatly strengthened the young country. The Constitution was signed by thirty-nine men,

John Lansing

Although thirty-nine delegates to the Constitutional Convention signed the U.S. Constitution, each state had to approve the Constitution in its own assembly before it was legally admitted as a state of the United States.

including Hamilton. The delegates decided that each former colony would become a state under the new Constitution the moment it approved the document.

Delaware became the first state on December 7, 1787. Soon Pennsylvania, New Jersey, Georgia, Connecticut, Massachusetts, Maryland, South Carolina, New Hampshire, and Virginia also became states by approving the Constitution.

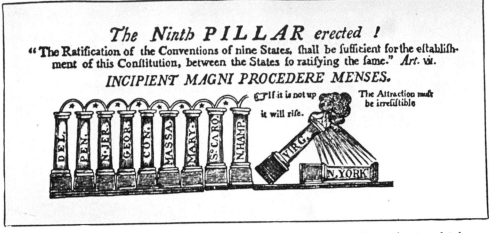

The Ninth *PILLAR* erected !

"The Ratification of the Conventions of nine States, shall be sufficient for the establishment of this Constitution, between the States so ratifying the same." *Art. vii.*

INCIPIENT MAGNI PROCEDERE MENSES.

This political cartoon, published in 1788, shows the order in which states approved the U.S. Constitution.

New York, however, did not immediately approve the new Constitution. Many New Yorkers disliked the idea of a stronger federal government. They felt that New York could do better on its own than as part of the United States. Many New Yorkers also felt that a Bill of Rights should be added to the Constitution to protect certain basic rights of individuals.

New Yorkers were split on the issue of statehood. Finally, in the summer of 1788, a convention was held in Poughkeepsie, New York, to determine whether New York would accept the Constitution. The entire nation closely followed the proceedings. It would have been a great blow to the country if a major state such as New York voted against the Constitution.

It appeared at first that the vote would go against the document, but Alexander Hamilton convinced many of the delegates to support it. In a breathtakingly close vote on July 26, 1788, the delegates voted 30–27 to accept the United States Constitution, and New York became the nation's eleventh state.

From January 11, 1785 to August 12, 1790, New York City was the nation's capital. George Washington's inauguration as the country's first president was held in the city on April 30, 1789. On the second-floor balcony of Federal Hall, at Wall and Broad streets, Washington took the oath of office, saying, "I do solemnly swear that I will faithfully execute the office of the President of the United States and will, to the best of my ability, preserve, protect, and defend the Constitution of the United States." Then he leaned down, kissed the Bible, and added, "So help me, God!"

When he became president, Washington lived in the presidential mansion at 3 Cherry Street. That site is now covered by a pier of the Brooklyn Bridge. Washington later moved to a larger mansion at 39 Broadway.

New York City remained the capital of the United States until 1790, when Philadelphia became the capital. In 1791 the United States added ten amendments to the Constitution—the Bill of Rights—which New Yorkers wanted

George Washington, on the balcony of Federal Hall in New York, being sworn in as president, April 30, 1789

included to protect individual rights. By that time New York's population and its manufacturing businesses were increasing so rapidly that the state was well on its way to becoming the seat of the American empire, just as George Washington had predicted.

View of New York's old City Hall on Wall Street in the late 1780s

JOHN JAY (1745–1829)

John Jay, America's first Supreme Court Justice, was born into a wealthy Dutch and French family in New York City. Jay spent his childhood on his family's estate at nearby Rye, New York. Jay was so advanced that by age six he was studying Latin. When he was almost seven, his father wrote, "Johnny is [very serious] and takes to learning exceedingly well."

In 1760, at the age of fourteen, Jay entered King's College, now Columbia University, which had been founded in New York City in 1754. He earned a reputation as a fair, honest, intelligent, and gentle young man. After his graduation he became a lawyer.

Jay favored the Loyalists until 1773. Disturbed by the continuing British taxation, he became a patriot. In 1774, he was elected to represent New York at the First Continental Congress, and the next year, he represented the colony at the Second Continental Congress. After Congress advised the colonies to organize themselves as states, Jay wrote New York's first state constitution in 1777. He was elected president of the Continental Congress in 1778 and served for about a year.

Jay served his country in many ways during the next few years. He went to Spain to obtain the help of the Spanish during the Revolutionary War. He helped negotiate the Treaty of Paris, which ended the Revolutionary War in 1783. He wrote five of the *Federalist* essays supporting the U.S. Constitution, and he helped Alexander Hamilton convince New York to approve the Constitution.

When the federal government was being organized, President Washington offered John Jay his choice of office. Thinking that the United States needed a strong court system, Jay chose to become the first Chief Justice of the Supreme Court. During his five years in office (1790–1795), Jay helped establish procedures for the Supreme Court. In 1795 he was elected governor of New York and served until 1801. Jay, who had once pledged that he "would risk all for independence" from Great Britain, died on his farm at the age of eighty-three.

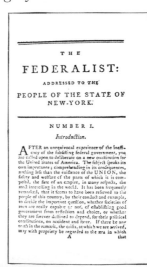

ALEXANDER HAMILTON (1757?-1804)

Alexander Hamilton was born on Nevis, a Caribbean island colonized by the British. When he was about five years old, his father's business failed, and the family moved to the nearby island of St. Croix. When Hamilton was about eight, his father abandoned the family. Several years later Alexander's mother died, and he went to live with a wealthy aunt and uncle on St. Croix.

A minister on St. Croix, named Hugh Knox, encouraged Hamilton's interest in learning. Certain that Hamilton was a genius, the minister advised Alexander's aunt and uncle to send him to college in America or Europe. But college was expensive, so instead twelve-year-old Alexander was sent to work for Nicholas Cruger, a wealthy merchant.

Young Hamilton worked every day for Cruger, but he spent every night reading and studying. Cruger was so impressed by Hamilton's work that he soon placed the boy in charge of a branch office on the other side of St. Croix. When Cruger went to America for half a year, he left fifteen-year-old Hamilton in charge of the business. Upon his return, Cruger spoke of making Hamilton a partner, but the young man still dreamed of going to college in America.

In the summer of 1772, the island of St. Croix was battered by a tremendous hurricane. Hamilton heroically helped save his aunt and uncle's house. At Reverend Knox's suggestion, Alexander wrote a story about the hurricane. His article was printed in a newspaper that was widely read throughout the British Caribbean islands. Hamilton's relatives were now convinced that he deserved to go to college. With Cruger's help they raised enough money to send him to America for an education.

Hamilton said good-bye to his relatives and friends and sailed to New York in 1772. For a year he attended a school in Elizabethtown (now Elizabeth), New Jersey. Then in the fall of 1773, he entered New York City's King's College, which is now Columbia University.

While Hamilton was in college, Americans were arguing about whether or not to rebel against England. He sided with the American patriots. After the Boston Tea Party, he wrote a newspaper article entitled "Defense of the Destruction of the Tea." That article was the first of many Hamilton wrote on behalf of the patriots' cause. He also made speeches at protest meetings. People were astounded that a seventeen-year-old youth could speak and write so eloquently, and soon his name was known to the American leaders.

Hamilton learned military tactics from books, and when the Revolution broke out, he was made captain of a New York artillery company. He

drilled his men into one of New York's finest fighting units. He led them in battles in New York and New Jersey. George Washington liked what he heard about young Hamilton, and in the spring of 1777, Washington made him his personal aide.

The commander-in-chief depended on the young man in many ways. Hamilton helped him write letters to the Continental Congress, and he helped Washington organize his army. Hamilton also fought in the Battle of Yorktown, the last major battle of the Revolution.

At the war's end, Hamilton moved to Albany, where he became a lawyer. In 1783 he settled in New York City and opened a Wall Street law office.

Hamilton soon earned a reputation as one of the best lawyers in the colonies and one of the great boosters of a stronger federal government.

Alexander Hamilton played a leading role in the creation and adoption of our federal Constitution. He was one of the main organizers of the Constitutional Convention that met in Philadelphia in 1787. He signed the Constitution as New York's representative and wrote 51 of the 85 famous *Federalist* essays urging adoption of the Constitution. And he was largely responsible for convincing New York lawmakers to approve the Constitution on July 26, 1788.

After George Washington was elected first president, he named Alexander Hamilton first secretary of the treasury. During his more than five years as treasury secretary, Hamilton strengthened U.S. finances and helped organize the nation's banking system. In 1796 he wrote much of George Washington's famous Farewell Address for the retiring first president.

For the last few years of his life, Hamilton practiced law in New York City. He was very outspoken about important political issues, and he made several political enemies. One of them was Aaron Burr, whom Hamilton prevented from becoming president of the United States.

In 1804, Hamilton also prevented Burr's being elected governor of New York. Burr challenged Hamilton to a duel. According to some reports, Hamilton was so upset over his son's recent death and his daughter's mental illness that he made no attempt to fire his gun. Burr shot Hamilton, who died the next day, on July 12. A portrait of Alexander Hamilton, the man who helped create the Constitution and who was the first secretary of the treasury, can be seen on the ten-dollar bills of the United States.

The Schaghen letter, announcing the purchase of Manhattan Island

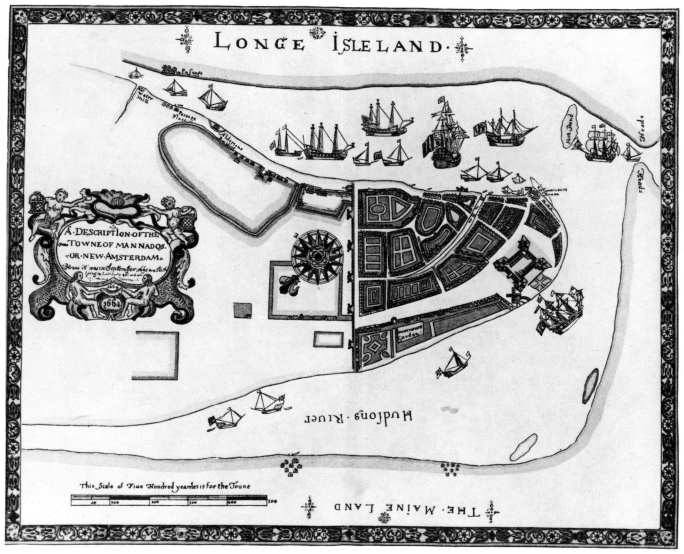

British map of Mannados (Manhattan), New York

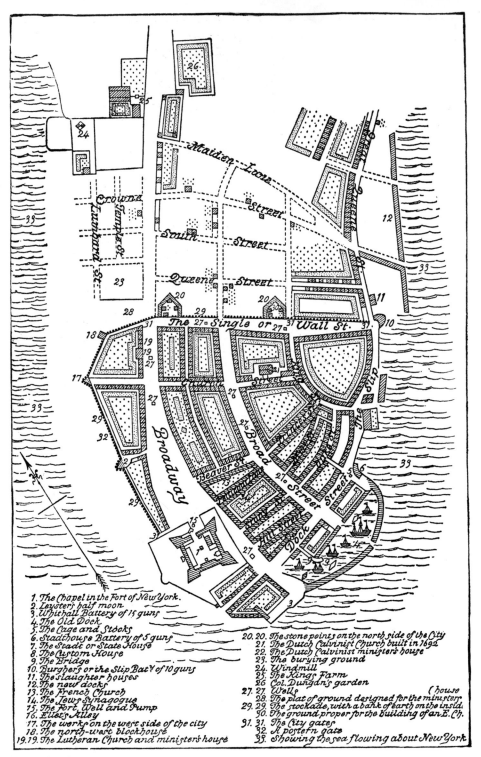

1. The Chapel in the Fort of New York.
2. Leyster's half moon
3. Whithall Battery of 15 guns
4. The Old Dock
5. The Cage and Stocks
6. Stadthouse Battery of 5 guns
7. The Stadt or State House
8. The Custom House
9. The Bridge
10. Burghers or the Slip Batty of 10 guns
11. The slaughter houses
12. The new docks
13. The French Church
14. The Jews Synagogue
15. The Fort, Well and Pump
16. Ellet's Alley
17. The works on the west side of the city
18. The north-west blockhouse
19.19. The Lutheran Church and ministers house

20.20. The stone points on the north side of the City
21. The Dutch Calvinist Church built in 1692
22. The Dutch Calvinist ministers house
23. The burying ground
24. Windmill
25. The Kings Farm
26. Col. Dungan's garden
27.27. Wells
28. The plat of ground designed for the minister's house
29.29. The stockade, with a bank of earth on the inside
30. The ground proper for the building of an E. Ch.
31.31. The City gates
32. A postern gate
33. Showing the sea flowing about New York

Map of New York in 1695

By his Excellency

William Cosby, Captain General and Governour in Chief of the Provinces of *New-York*, *New-Jersey*, and Territories thereon depending, in America, Vice-Admiral of the same, and Colonel in His Majesty's Army.

A PROCLAMATION.

WHereas by the Contrivance of some evil Disposed and Disaffected Persons, divers Journals or Printed News Papers, (entitled, *The New-York Weekly Journal, containing the freshest Advices, Foreign and Domestick*) have been caused to be Printed and Published by *John Peter Zenger*, in many of which Journals or Printed News-Papers (but more particularly those Numbred 7, 47, 48, 49) are contained divers Scandalous, Virulent, False and Seditious Reflections, not only upon the whole Legislature, in general, and upon the most considerable Persons in the most distinguish'd Stations in this Province, but also upon His Majesty's lawful and rightful Government, and just Prerogative. Which said Reflections seem contrived by the wicked Authors of them, not only to create Jealousies, Discontents and Animosities in the Minds of his Majesty's Leige People of this Province, to the Subversion of the Peace & Tranquility thereof, but to alienate their Affections from the best of Kings, and raise *Factions*, *Tumults* and *Sedition* among them. *Wherefore* I have thought fit, by and with the Advice of His Majesty's Council, to issue this Proclamation, hereby Promising a Reward of *Fifty Pounds* to such Person or Persons who shall discover the Author or Authors of the said *Scandalous*, *Virulent* and *Seditious Reflections* contained in the said *Journals* or *Printed News-Papers*, to be paid to the Person or Persons discovering the same, as soon as such Author or Authors shall be Convicted of having been the Author or Authors thereof.

GIVEN under My Hand and Seal at Fort-George in New-York this Sixth Day of November, in the Eighth year of the Reign of Our Sovereign Lord GEORGE the Second, by the Grace of GOD, of Great-Britain, France and Ireland, KING Defender of the Faith, &c. and in the Year of Our LORD 1734.

By his Excellency's Command,
 Fred. Morris, D. Cl. Conc.

W. COSBY

GOD Save the KING.

Proclamation issued against John Peter Zenger

THE
New - York Weekly JOURNAL

Containing the freſheſt Advices, Foreign, and Domeſtick.

MUNDAY November 25th, 1734.

To all my Subſcribers and Benefactors who take my weekly Journall.

Gentlemen, Ladies and Others;

AS you laſt week were Diſappointed of my Journall, I think it Incumbent upon me, to publiſh my Apoligy which is this. On the Lords Day, the Seventeenth of this Inſtant, I was Arreſted, taken and Impriſoned in the common Goal of this City, by Virtue of a Warrant from the *Governour*, and the Honorable *Franciſs Harriſon*, Eſq; and others in Councill of which (God willing) yo'l have a Coppy, whereupon I was put under ſuch Reſtraint that I had not the Liberty of Pen Ink, or Paper, or to ſee, or ſpeak with People, till upon my Complaint to the Honourable the Chief Juſtice, at my appearing before him upon my *Habias Corpus* on the *Wedneſday* following, Who diſcountenanced that Proceeding, and therefore I have had ſince that Time, the Liberty of Speaking through the Hole of the Door, to my Wife and Servants by which I doubt not yo'l think me ſufficiently Excuſed for not ſending my laſt weeks *Journall*; and I hope for the future by the Liberty of Speaking to my Servants thro the Hole of the Door of the Priſon, to entertain you with my weokly *Journal* as formerly. *And am your obliged Humble Servant,* *J. Peter Zenger.*

Mr. *Zenger*;

AS the Liberty of the Preſs is juſtly eſteemed and univerſally acknowledged by Engliſhmen, to be the grand Paladium of all their Liberties, which Liberty of the Preſs, I have rejoyced to ſee well defended in Sundry of your Papers, and particularly by your No. 2. 3. 10. 11. 15. 16. 17. 18. 24. & 54. and by an annonimous Authors Obſervations on the chief Juſtices Charge of *January* laſt; now, for ſo much as it may not only be of preſent Uſe, but of future Advantage, that ſuch Matters of Fact, that concern the Liberty of the Preſs, may be faithfully recorded and tranſmitted to Poſterity, therefore I have ſent you a Detail of ſuch particulars that concern the Liberty of the Preſs within this Colony, and becauſe I would not have you or my ſelf charged with the Publication of a Libel, I ſhall confine my ſelf to a plain Narration of Facts without any comments.

On Tueſday the 15th of *Octo.* 1734. *The ſupream Court of* New-York, *began, when the Honourable* James De Lancey, *Eſq; Cheif Juſtie charged the Grand Jury. The Conclusion of which Charge was as follows.*

Gentlemen, I ſhall conclude with reading a Paragraph or two out of the ſame Book, † concerning Libels; they are arrived to that height, that they call

IN CONGRESS, JULY 4, 1776

The unanimous Declaration of the thirteen united States of America,

When in the Course of human events, it becomes necessary for one people to dissolve the political bands which have connected them with another, and to assume among the powers of the earth, the separate and equal station to which the Laws of Nature and of Nature's God entitle them, a decent respect to the opinions of mankind requires that they should declare the causes which impel them to the separation. — We hold these truths to be self-evident, that all men are created equal, that they are endowed by their Creator with certain unalienable Rights, that among these are Life, Liberty and the pursuit of Happiness. — That to secure these rights, Governments are instituted among Men, deriving their just powers from the consent of the governed. — That whenever any Form of Government becomes destructive of these ends, it is the Right of the People to alter or to abolish it, and to institute new Government, laying its foundation on such principles and organizing its powers in such form, as to them shall seem most likely to effect their Safety and Happiness. Prudence, indeed, will dictate that Governments long established should not be changed for light and transient causes; and accordingly all experience hath shewn, that mankind are more disposed to suffer, while evils are sufferable, than to right themselves by abolishing the forms to which they are accustomed. But when a long train of abuses and usurpations, pursuing invariably the same Object evinces a design to reduce them under absolute Despotism, it is their right, it is their duty, to throw off such Government, and to provide new Guards for their future security. — Such has been the patient sufferance of these Colonies; and such is now the necessity which constrains them to alter their former Systems of Government. The history of the present King of Great Britain is a history of repeated injuries and usurpations, all having in direct object the establishment of an absolute Tyranny over these States. To prove this, let Facts be submitted to a candid world. — He has refused his Assent to Laws, the most wholesome and necessary for the public good. — He has forbidden his Governors to pass Laws of immediate and pressing importance, unless suspended in their operation till his Assent should be obtained; and when so suspended, he has utterly neglected to attend to them. — He has refused to pass other Laws for the accommodation of large districts of people, unless those people would relinquish the right of Representation in the Legislature, a right inestimable to them and formidable to tyrants only. — He has called together legislative bodies at places unusual, uncomfortable, and distant from the depository of their public Records, for the sole purpose of fatiguing them into compliance with his measures. — He has dissolved Representative Houses repeatedly, for opposing with manly firmness his invasions on the rights of the people. — He has refused for a long time, after such dissolutions, to cause others to be elected; whereby the Legislative powers, incapable of Annihilation, have returned to the People at large for their exercise; the State remaining in the mean time exposed to all the dangers of invasion from without, and convulsions within. — He has endeavoured to prevent the population of these States; for that purpose obstructing the Laws for Naturalization of Foreigners; refusing to pass others to encourage their migrations hither, and raising the conditions of new Appropriations of Lands. — He has obstructed the Administration of Justice, by refusing his Assent to Laws for establishing Judiciary powers. — He has made Judges dependent on his Will alone, for the tenure of their offices, and the amount and payment of their salaries. — He has erected a multitude of New Offices, and sent hither swarms of Officers to harrass our people, and eat out their substance. — He has kept among us, in times of peace, Standing Armies without the Consent of our legislatures. — He has affected to render the Military independent of and superior to the Civil power. — He has combined with others to subject us to a jurisdiction foreign to our constitution, and unacknowledged by our laws; giving his Assent to their Acts of pretended Legislation: — For Quartering large bodies of armed troops among us: — For protecting them, by a mock Trial, from punishment for any Murders which they should commit on the Inhabitants of these States: — For cutting off our Trade with all parts of the world: — For imposing Taxes on us without our Consent: — For depriving us in many cases, of the benefits of Trial by Jury: — For transporting us beyond Seas to be tried for pretended offences: — For abolishing the free System of English Laws in a neighbouring Province, establishing therein an Arbitrary government, and enlarging its Boundaries so as to render it at once an example and fit instrument for introducing the same absolute rule into these Colonies: — For taking away our Charters, abolishing our most valuable Laws, and altering fundamentally the Forms of our Governments: — For suspending our own Legislatures, and declaring themselves invested with power to legislate for us in all cases whatsoever. — He has abdicated Government here, by declaring us out of his Protection and waging War against us. — He has plundered our seas, ravaged our Coasts, burnt our towns, and destroyed the lives of our people. — He is at this time transporting large Armies of foreign Mercenaries to compleat the works of death, desolation and tyranny, already begun with circumstances of Cruelty & perfidy scarcely paralleled in the most barbarous ages, and totally unworthy the Head of a civilized nation. — He has constrained our fellow Citizens taken Captive on the high Seas to bear Arms against their Country, to become the executioners of their friends and Brethren, or to fall themselves by their Hands. — He has excited domestic insurrections amongst us, and has endeavoured to bring on the inhabitants of our frontiers, the merciless Indian Savages, whose known rule of warfare, is an undistinguished destruction of all ages, sexes and conditions. In every stage of these Oppressions We have Petitioned for Redress in the most humble terms: Our repeated Petitions have been answered only by repeated injury. A Prince whose character is thus marked by every act which may define a Tyrant, is unfit to be the ruler of a free people. Nor have We been wanting in attentions to our Brittish brethren. We have warned them from time to time of attempts by their legislature to extend an unwarrantable jurisdiction over us. We have reminded them of the circumstances of our emigration and settlement here. We have appealed to their native justice and magnanimity, and we have conjured them by the ties of our common kindred to disavow these usurpations, which, would inevitably interrupt our connections and correspondence. They too have been deaf to the voice of justice and of consanguinity. We must, therefore, acquiesce in the necessity, which denounces our Separation, and hold them, as we hold the rest of mankind, Enemies in War, in Peace Friends. —

We, therefore, the Representatives of the united States of America, in General Congress, Assembled, appealing to the Supreme Judge of the world for the rectitude of our intentions, do, in the Name, and by Authority of the good People of these Colonies, solemnly publish and declare, That these United Colonies are, and of Right ought to be Free and Independent States; that they are Absolved from all Allegiance to the British Crown, and that all political connection between them and the State of Great Britain, is and ought to be totally dissolved; and that as Free and Independent States, they have full Power to levy War, conclude Peace, contract Alliances, establish Commerce, and to do all other Acts and Things which Independent States may of right do. — And for the support of this Declaration, with a firm reliance on the protection of divine Providence, we mutually pledge to each other our Lives, our Fortunes and our sacred Honor.

John Hancock

Button Gwinnett
Lyman Hall
Geo Walton.

Wm Hooper
Joseph Hewes,
John Penn

Edward Rutledge.

Thos Heyward Junr.
Thomas Lynch Junr.
Arthur Middleton

Samuel Chase
Wm Paca
Thos Stone
Charles Carroll of Carrollton

George Wythe
Richard Henry Lee
Th Jefferson
Benja Harrison
Ths Nelson jr.
Francis Lightfoot Lee
Carter Braxton

Robt Morris
Benjamin Rush
Benja Franklin
John Morton
Geo Clymer
Jas Smith
Geo Taylor
James Wilson
Geo Ross
Caesar Rodney
Geo Read
Tho M:Kean

Wm Floyd
Phil Livingston
Frans Lewis
Lewis Morris

Richd Stockton
Jno Witherspoon
Fras Hopkinson
John Hart
Abra Clark

Josiah Bartlett
Wm Whipple
Saml Adams
John Adams
Robt Treat Paine
Elbridge Gerry
Step Hopkins
William Ellery
Roger Sherman
Sam el Huntington
Wm Williams
Oliver Wolcott
Matthew Thornton

Colonial America Time Line

Before the arrival of Europeans, many millions of Indians belonging to dozens of tribes lived in North America (and also in Central and South America)

About 982 A.D.—Eric the Red, born in Norway, reaches Greenland during one of the first European voyages to North America

About 985—Eric the Red brings settlers from Iceland to Greenland

About 1000—Leif Ericson (Eric the Red's son) leads what is thought to be the first European expedition to mainland North America; Leif probably lands in Canada

1492—Christopher Columbus, sailing for Spain, reaches America

1497—John Cabot reaches Canada in the first English voyage to North America

1513—Ponce de León of Spain explores Florida

1519-1521—Hernando Cortés of Spain conquers Mexico

1565—St. Augustine, Florida, the first permanent European town in what is now the United States, is founded by the Spanish

1607—Jamestown, Virginia is founded, the first permanent English town in the present-day U.S.

1608—Frenchman Samuel de Champlain founds the village of Quebec, Canada

1609—Henry Hudson explores the eastern coast of present-day U.S. for The Netherlands; the Dutch then claim parts of New York, New Jersey, Delaware, and Connecticut and name the area New Netherland

1619—Virginia's House of Burgesses, America's first representative lawmaking body, is founded

1619—The first shipment of black slaves arrives in Jamestown

1620—English Pilgrims found Massachusetts' first permanent town at Plymouth

1621—Massachusetts Pilgrims and Indians hold the famous first Thanksgiving feast in colonial America

1622—Indians kill 347 settlers in Virginia

1623—Colonization of New Hampshire is begun by the English

1624—Colonization of present-day New York State is begun by the Dutch at Fort Orange (Albany)

1625—The Dutch start building New Amsterdam (now New York City)

1630—The town of Boston, Massachusetts is founded by the English Puritans

1633—Colonization of Connecticut is begun by the English

1634—Colonization of Maryland is begun by the English

1635—Boston Latin School, the colonies' first public school, is founded

1636—Harvard, the colonies' first college, is founded in Massachusetts

1636—Rhode Island colonization begins when Englishman Roger Williams founds Providence

1638—The colonies' first library is established at Harvard

1638—Delaware colonization begins when Swedish people build Fort Christina at present-day Wilmington

1640—Stephen Daye of Cambridge, Massachusetts prints *The Bay Psalm Book*, the first English-language book published in what is now the U.S.

1643—Swedish settlers begin colonizing Pennsylvania

1647—Massachusetts forms the first public school system in the colonies

1650—North Carolina is colonized by Virginia settlers in about this year

1650—Population of colonial U.S. is about 50,000

1660—New Jersey colonization is begun by the Dutch at present-day Jersey City

1670—South Carolina colonization is begun by the English near Charleston

1673—Jacques Marquette and Louis Jolliet explore the upper Mississippi River for France

1675-76—New England colonists beat Indians in King Philip's War

1682—Philadelphia, Pennsylvania is settled

1682—La Salle explores Mississippi River all the way to its mouth in Louisiana and claims the whole Mississippi Valley for France

1693—College of William and Mary is founded in Williamsburg, Virginia

1700—Colonial population is about 250,000

1704—*The Boston News-Letter*, the first successful newspaper in the colonies, is founded

1706—Benjamin Franklin is born in Boston

1732—George Washington, future first president of the United States, is born in Virginia

1733—English begin colonizing Georgia, their thirteenth colony in what is now the United States

1735—John Adams, future second president, is born in Massachusetts

1743—Thomas Jefferson, future third president, is born in Virginia

1750—Colonial population is about 1,200,000

1754—France and England begin fighting the French and Indian War over North American lands

1763—England, victorious in the war, gains Canada and most other French lands east of the Mississippi River

1764—British pass Sugar Act to gain tax money from the colonists

1765—British pass the Stamp Act, which the colonists despise; colonists then hold the Stamp Act Congress in New York City

1766—British repeal the Stamp Act

1770—British soldiers kill five Americans in the "Boston Massacre"

1773—Colonists dump British tea into Boston Harbor at the "Boston Tea Party"

1774—British close up port of Boston to punish the city for the tea party

1774—Delegates from all the colonies but Georgia meet in Philadelphia at the First Continental Congress

1775—April 19: Revolutionary war begins at Lexington and Concord, Massachusetts

  May 10: Second Continental Congress convenes in Philadelphia

  June 17: Colonists inflict heavy losses on British but lose Battle of Bunker Hill near Boston

  July 3: George Washington takes command of Continental army

1776—March 17: Washington's troops force the British out of Boston in the first major American win of the war

  May 4: Rhode Island is first colony to declare itself independent of Britain

July 4: Declaration of Independence is adopted

December 26: Washington's forces win Battle of Trenton (New Jersey)

1777—January 3: Americans win at Princeton, New Jersey

August 16: Americans win Battle of Bennington at New York-Vermont border

September 11: British win Battle of Brandywine Creek near Philadelphia

September 26: British capture Philadelphia

October 4: British win Battle of Germantown near Philadelphia

October 17: About 5,000 British troops surrender at Battle of Saratoga in New York

December 19: American army goes into winter quarters at Valley Forge, Pennsylvania, where more than 3,000 of them die by spring

1778—February 6: France joins the American side

July 4: American George Rogers Clark captures Kaskaskia, Illinois from the British

1779—February 23-25: George Rogers Clark captures Vincennes in Indiana

September 23: American John Paul Jones captures British ship *Serapis*

1780—May 12: British take Charleston, South Carolina

August 16: British badly defeat Americans at Camden, South Carolina

October 7: Americans defeat British at Kings Mountain, South Carolina

1781—January 17: Americans win battle at Cowpens, South Carolina

March 1: Articles of Confederation go into effect as laws of the United States

March 15: British suffer heavy losses at Battle of Guilford Courthouse in North Carolina; British then give up most of North Carolina

October 19: British army under Charles Cornwallis surrenders at Yorktown, Virginia as major revolutionary war fighting ends

1783—September 3: United States officially wins Revolution as the United States and Great Britain sign Treaty of Paris

November 25: Last British troops leave New York City

1787—On December 7, Delaware becomes the first state by approving the U.S. Constitution

1788—On June 21, New Hampshire becomes the ninth state when it approves the U.S. Constitution; with nine states having approved it, the Constitution goes into effect as the law of the United States

1789—On April 30, George Washington is inaugurated as first president of the United States

1790—On May 29, Rhode Island becomes the last of the original thirteen colonies to become a state

1791—U.S. Bill of Rights goes into effect on December 15

INDEX- *Page numbers in **boldface** type indicate illustrations.*

About the Author

Dennis Fradin attended Northwestern University on a partial creative scholarship and was graduated in 1967. He has published stories and articles in such places as *Ingenue*, *The Saturday Evening Post*, *Scholastic*, *Chicago*, *Oui*, and *National Humane Review*. His previous books include the Young People's Stories of Our States series for Childrens Press, and *Bad Luck Tony* for Prentice-Hall. In the True Book series Dennis has written about astronomy, farming, comets, archaeology, movies, space colonies, the space lab, explorers, and pioneers. He is married and the father of three children.

Photo Credits

The Bettmann Archive—11 (top), 14, 20, 25, 29, 33, 61, 62, 75 (right), 77, 80, 84 (bottom), 86, 96, 97, 104, 106, 138, 140

Frick Art Reference Library—128

Historical Pictures Service, Chicago—31, 37, 39, 41, 48 (2 photos), 50, 55, 57, 58, 71, 72, 78, 83 (top), 89, 94 (top), 101, 103, 104, 122, 123, 125, 127, 136, 137, 142 (left), 146, 147, 149, 150

Image Finders/ © Anne Data—7 (bottom)

Library of Congress—115, 117, 141, 151

Morristown Historical Park—121

Museum of the American Indian—17 (2 photos), 18

National Gallery of Canada, Ottawa—132

Newberry Library—75

New Hampshire Historical Society—94 (bottom)

The New York Public Library—22 (top), 35, 119

Northwind Picture Archives—12, 22 (bottom), 23, 26, 27, 28, 37, 45, 53, 54, 60, 69, 74, 76, 85, 90, 107, 108, 109, 111, 116, 118, 120, 129, 130, 133, 134, 142 (right), 144, 148

UPI/Bettmann Newsphotos—4, 7 (top), 8, 11 (2 center photos and bottom)

Horizon Graphics, 5 (map)

Cover and Interior Design—Horizon Graphics

Cover art—Steven Dobson